REASONING
SKILLS
SUCCESS
IN 20 MINUTES
A DAY

REASONING SKILLS SUCCESS
IN 20 MINUTES A DAY

2nd Edition

LEARNINGEXPRESS®

NEW YORK

Library of Congress Cataloging-in-Publication Data:
    Reasoning skills success in 20 minutes a day.—2nd ed.
        p. cm.
    ISBN 1-57685-493-0
    1. Reasoning (Psychology) I. Title: Reasoning skills success in twenty minutes a day.
    II. Title.
BF442.C48 2005
153.4'3—dc22

                                                                        2005047185

Printed in the United States of America

9 8 7 6 5 4 3 2

Second Edition

ISBN 1-57685-493-0

For information on LearningExpress, other LearningExpress products, or bulk sales, please write to us at:
    LearningExpress
    55 Broadway
    8th Floor
    New York, NY 10006

Or visit us at:
    www.learnatest.com

Contents

CONTENTS

CONTENTS

How to Use This Book ▶

This book is designed to help you improve your critical thinking and reasoning skills in 20 short lessons of 20 minutes a day. If you read one chapter a day, Monday through Friday, and do all the exercises carefully, you should see dramatic improvement in your ability to think critically and to solve problems logically and effectively by the end of your month of study.

Although each lesson is designed to be a skill builder on its own, it is important that you proceed through this book in order, from Lesson 1 through Lesson 20. Like most other skills, critical thinking and reasoning develop in layers. Each lesson in this book builds upon the ideas discussed in those before it.

Each lesson provides several exercises that give you the opportunity to practice the skills you learn throughout the book. To help you be sure you're on the right track, you'll also find answers and explanations for these exercise sets. Each lesson also provides practical suggestions for how to continue practicing the taught skills throughout the rest of the day and week—and the rest of your life. In addition, two special review lessons go over the key skills and concepts in each half of the book and provide you with practice applying them in practical, real-life situations.

To help you gauge your progress, this book contains a pretest and a posttest. You should take the pretest *before* you start Lesson 1. Then, after you've finished Lesson 20, take the posttest. The tests contain different questions but assess the same skills, so you will be able to see how much your critical thinking and reasoning skills have improved after completing the lessons in this book.

▶ Be an Active Listener and Observer

To make the most of this text, it's important to remember that critical thinking and reasoning skills are necessary for just about every aspect of life—whether personal, professional, or academic. That's why it's so important to become an *active listener and observer.*

People often come to conclusions based on what they think or feel rather than on the *evidence* before them. They make decisions based on what they *want* to hear rather than what is really being said; they take action based on what they *imagine* to be true rather than what is actually the case. But by really listening to what people say and *how* they say it (facial expressions and tone often say much more than words themselves), you help ensure that you will be reacting to what's really being said, not just to what you want to hear.

Similarly, by paying careful attention to and thinking critically about every situation, you'll help ensure that the decisions you make and the conclusions you come to will be justified. For example, if a place looks unsavory to you, analyze what it is about that place that makes you uncomfortable. Feelings generally come from things we are able to sense, even subconsciously, in our environment. The more you can point to as justification for your thoughts, feelings, and actions, the more logical your decisions and actions will be.

Much of this book will be devoted to helping you build your observation skills. Meanwhile, here are a few pointers to help you not only as you work through this book, but in everything you do.

Keep an Open Mind

It is very rarely the case that there is only *one* possible answer to a problem or only *one* "right" way to think or act. Even in math, where things seem to be black and white, there is usually more than one way to solve a problem. When it comes to making decisions, especially those that involve other people, remember that between black and white, there are a thousand shades of gray. You may prefer one shade over another, but that doesn't necessarily cancel out the other colors.

Consider All Sides

It is easy to make the mistake of coming to a conclusion or making a decision before all sides of an argument are heard. However, the more complete a picture you can get of a given situation, the more effective your decision or solution will be. To that end, listen to all sides of an argument, and examine a situation from various points of view. If you do, your decisions will be much more sound and you'll be able to solve problems more effectively.

Separate Feelings from Facts

This book will address, in more detail, the difference between fact and opinion later on, but the distinction is so important that it's worth mentioning now. What most often clouds people's ability to reason effectively is their emotions. Indeed, this is a natural tendency, but if you give feelings precedence over reason, you often end up making poor decisions. This is not to say that you shouldn't consider your feelings—of course you should—but just be sure they're not overriding the facts.

Think before You Act

People are often under pressure to make quick decisions. But with the exception of emergency situations, it's usually best to take time to reason things through. Hasty decisions are less productive in the long run because they're usually not the most logical or informed decisions. If you take a little time to consider all sides and separate feelings from facts, you're much more likely to make a wise decision or find an effective solution.

Of course, sometimes making a quick decision is the only option, like when taking a timed test or in an emergency situation. That's why it's so important to build your reasoning skills now and make them a part of your everyday thought process. Then when you are pressed for time, you'll be able to reason through the situation quickly and effectively.

If any of this sounds confusing, don't worry—each of these ideas will be explained thoroughly in the lessons that follow. What's important is that you work on developing these skills, starting with Lesson 1, "Critical Thinking and Reasoning Skills."

REASONING SKILLS
SUCCESS
IN 20 MINUTES
A DAY

Pretest

Before you start your study of reasoning skills, you may want to get an idea of how much you already know and how much you need to learn. If that's the case, take the pretest in this chapter.

The pretest consists of 35 multiple-choice questions that cover all the lessons in this book. Naturally, not all of the reasoning skills in this book are covered on the test. Even if you get all of the questions on the pretest right, you will undoubtedly profit from working through the lessons anyway; only a fraction of the information in this book is covered on the pretest. On the other hand, if you miss a lot of questions on the pretest, don't despair. These lessons are designed to teach you critical thinking and reasoning skills step by step. Just take your time and enjoy the learning process.

If you get a high score on this pretest, you may be able to spend less time working through this book than you originally planned. If you get a low score, you may find that you will need more than 20 minutes a day to get through each chapter and learn all about logical reasoning.

On the next page, there's an answer sheet you can use to fill in your answer choices. Or, if you prefer, simply circle the correct answer underneath the item itself. If the book doesn't belong to you, write the numbers 1–35 on a piece of paper and record your answers there. Take as much time as you need to complete this short test. When you finish, check your answers against the answer key at the end of this chapter. Each answer tells you which chapter of this book teaches you about the reasoning skill in that question.

1.	ⓐ	ⓑ	ⓒ	ⓓ
2.	ⓐ	ⓑ	ⓒ	ⓓ
3.	ⓐ	ⓑ	ⓒ	ⓓ
4.	ⓐ	ⓑ	ⓒ	ⓓ
5.	ⓐ	ⓑ	ⓒ	ⓓ
6.	ⓐ	ⓑ	ⓒ	ⓓ
7.	ⓐ	ⓑ	ⓒ	ⓓ
8.	ⓐ	ⓑ	ⓒ	ⓓ
9.	ⓐ	ⓑ	ⓒ	ⓓ
10.	ⓐ	ⓑ	ⓒ	ⓓ
11.	ⓐ	ⓑ	ⓒ	ⓓ
12.	ⓐ	ⓑ	ⓒ	ⓓ

13.	ⓐ	ⓑ	ⓒ	ⓓ
14.	ⓐ	ⓑ	ⓒ	ⓓ
15.	ⓐ	ⓑ	ⓒ	ⓓ
16.	ⓐ	ⓑ	ⓒ	ⓓ
17.	ⓐ	ⓑ	ⓒ	ⓓ
18.	ⓐ	ⓑ	ⓒ	ⓓ
19.	ⓐ	ⓑ	ⓒ	ⓓ
20.	ⓐ	ⓑ	ⓒ	ⓓ
21.	ⓐ	ⓑ	ⓒ	ⓓ
22.	ⓐ	ⓑ	ⓒ	ⓓ
23.	ⓐ	ⓑ	ⓒ	ⓓ
24.	ⓐ	ⓑ	ⓒ	ⓓ

25.	ⓐ	ⓑ	ⓒ	ⓓ
26.	ⓐ	ⓑ	ⓒ	ⓓ
27.	ⓐ	ⓑ	ⓒ	ⓓ
28.	ⓐ	ⓑ	ⓒ	ⓓ
29.	ⓐ	ⓑ	ⓒ	ⓓ
30.	ⓐ	ⓑ	ⓒ	ⓓ
31.	ⓐ	ⓑ	ⓒ	ⓓ
32.	ⓐ	ⓑ	ⓒ	ⓓ
33.	ⓐ	ⓑ	ⓒ	ⓓ
34.	ⓐ	ⓑ	ⓒ	ⓓ
35.	ⓐ	ⓑ	ⓒ	ⓓ

► Pretest

Read the following passage and then answer the questions that follow.

Wendy is a junior in high school and is getting ready to choose a college. She is a serious student and wants to go to the school with the best premed program. However, she doesn't want to be too far from home because she wants to be able to visit her sister, who has recently been in a serious accident, on a regular basis. Wendy is likely to obtain scholarships—perhaps even a full scholarship—but she is worried that her parents may not be able to afford whatever costs the scholarships don't cover.

1. Which of the following most accurately presents the issues Wendy must consider, in order of priority?
   a. academic reputation, financial aid, social life on campus
   b. location, financial aid, and academic reputation
   c. financial aid, student services, location
   d. academic reputation, campus environment, location

2. Which of the following is probably the best choice for Wendy?
   a. the community college, which offers Wendy a full scholarship and has a new but unranked premed track
   b. an expensive liberal arts college, ranked in the top ten for its premed program, which offers Wendy a three-quarters scholarship. The college is a ten-hour drive from Wendy's home.
   c. the state university, ranked in the top 20 for its premed program, which offers Wendy a full scholarship for her first two years and guarantees continued scholarships if she maintains at least a B+ grade point average. The state university is two hours away from Wendy's home.
   d. Put off school for a few years until Wendy can save up some money and her sister has recovered. This way, Wendy will be less limited in which school she can choose.

Choose the best answer for each of the following.

3. "There are 52 weeks in a year" is
   a. a fact.
   b. an opinion.
   c. probably a fact, but I'd have to verify it first.
   d. none of the above.

4. "Grand Canyon National Park encompasses more than 1.2 million acres" is
   a. a fact.
   b. an opinion.
   c. probably a fact, but I'd have to verify it first.
   d. none of the above.

5. "There's nothing better than a pepperoni pizza!" is
   a. a fact.
   b. an opinion.
   c. probably a fact, but I'd have to verify it first.
   d. none of the above.

The following items (6–20) present questions, statements, or short passages that illustrate the process of reasoning or critical thinking. In some items, the speaker's reasoning is flawed. Read each item and select the answer choice that most accurately describes it. Choose **d** if there is no flaw or if the speaker remains neutral.

6. "You don't mean you'd actually support that liar if he ran for re-election, do you?"
  a. The question is unclear and confusing.
  b. Inherent in the question is a bias against the politician.
  c. The question assumes the listener is going to vote.
  d. The speaker is remaining neutral.

7. "New GingerSnap Soda costs less!"
  a. The ad doesn't tell how much the soda costs.
  b. The ad doesn't tell how much other sodas cost.
  c. The ad doesn't tell what the soda costs less than.
  d. This ad is fine as it is.

8. "Come on, Janet. You're much too smart to pass up this opportunity! Besides, I know what a kind and generous person you are."
  a. The speaker is flattering Janet.
  b. The speaker is pressuring Janet.
  c. The speaker is trying to scare Janet.
  d. The speaker is remaining neutral.

9. "Either we put 40 students in each class or we hire two dozen new teachers. There's no other choice."
  a. The speaker is proposing two equally bad solutions.
  b. The speaker is trying to change the subject.
  c. The speaker isn't allowing for other possibilities, like staggering classes.
  d. There's nothing wrong with the speaker's reasoning.

10. "I wouldn't listen to what Charlie says about anything, and *especially* not what he says about politics. I mean, all he does is watch *Friends* reruns all day. What does he know?"
  a. The speaker assumes that Charlie can't have a valid opinion about politics because he watches *Friends* reruns.
  b. The speaker assumes that the listener will listen to Charlie in the first place.
  c. The speaker doesn't like *Friends* reruns.
  d. There's nothing wrong with the speaker's reasoning.

11. "I'm sorry I was late professor, it's just that I am really upset. I just found out that I didn't make the basketball team."
  a. The speaker is bragging.
  b. The speaker is trying to appeal to the professor's sense of pity.
  c. The speaker's excuse is too vague.
  d. The speaker is remaining neutral.

12. "You agree with me, don't you, Marlene? Well, if you don't, don't worry. The last person who disagreed with me only got fired."
  a. The speaker is using humor inappropriately.
  b. The speaker is trying to get Marlene fired.
  c. The speaker is trying to scare Marlene into agreeing with him.
  d. The speaker is remaining neutral.

13. "I didn't pass the entrance exam because the weather was so nice."
  a. The speaker has no credibility.
  b. The speaker is jumping to conclusions.
  c. The speaker's explanation is irrelevant to the claim.
  d. There's nothing wrong with the speaker's reasoning.

14. "Last year, I sprained my ankle jogging, so it is probably a dangerous sport."
   a. The speaker knows very little about dangerous sports.
   b. The speaker draws an unfair conclusion about the sport based on just one incident.
   c. The speaker is trying to convince others not to participate in the sport.
   d. There's nothing wrong with the speaker's reasoning.

15. "I was a really good student in music class, so I should make a great performer someday."
   a. The speaker is jumping to conclusions.
   b. The speaker's reasoning is untestable.
   c. The explanation is circular.
   d. There's nothing wrong with the speaker's reasoning.

16. "Let's not go out tonight, Abe. I'm really tired, we're trying to save money, and we have to get up early and work tomorrow. A relaxing night at home makes more sense."
   a. The speaker is trying to blame Abe for their problems.
   b. The speaker is trying to make Abe feel sorry for her.
   c. The speaker is biased.
   d. There's nothing wrong with the speaker's reasoning.

17. "If we let Roger stay out until midnight, next thing you know, he'll be coming in at one, then three, and then not at all."
   a. The speaker is assuming that Roger wants to stay out all night.
   b. The speaker is assuming that *X* will automatically lead to *Y*.
   c. The speaker is assuming that *X* and *Y* are unacceptable alternatives.
   d. There's nothing wrong with the speaker's reasoning.

18. "I didn't cheat on my taxes. I just used creative accounting techniques."
   a. The speaker is breaking the law.
   b. The speaker is setting a bad example for others.
   c. The speaker is using a slanted phrase for "cheating."
   d. There's nothing wrong with the speaker's reasoning.

19. "I know I didn't do a great job on my paper, Professor Lang. But look at how many students cheated on the exam!"
   a. The student is bringing in an irrelevant issue.
   b. The student is blaming other students for her problems.
   c. The student is making a circular argument.
   d. There's nothing wrong with the speaker's reasoning.

20. "Hey, Todd, check this out! Two weeks ago, I bought this good luck charm, and I've been carrying it around with me every day. Since then, I found $20 in the street, I got the apartment I was hoping for, *and* I got a date with Cindy! This good luck charm really works!"
   a. The speaker doesn't believe in good luck charms.
   b. The speaker is assuming that the good luck charm is responsible for his string of good luck.
   c. The speaker doesn't provide enough evidence that the charm works.
   d. There's nothing wrong with the speaker's reasoning.

In the following situations, which source is most credible?

21. Regarding the authenticity of a fifty-dollar bill
   a. a professor of American history
   b. a counterfeiter
   c. a wealthy person
   d. an official with the Bureau of Engraving and Printing (BEP), one of the bureaus of the U.S. Treasury

22. In defense of a boy accused of stealing from a classmate
   a. his mother
   b. the principal
   c. his teacher
   d. his best friend

Read the following argument carefully and answer the questions that follow.

(1) Although many high-school students might disagree, it should be a requirement that they complete ninety hours of community service in order to graduate. (2) Ninety hours may seem like a long time, but stretched out over the course of three or four years, it's a very feasible goal. (3) Participating in community service improves self-confidence and provides students with the skills needed to analyze and solve real-world problems. (4) For instance, students might choose to volunteer for an organization that aims to improve literacy in adults.
(5) There are not many in-school educational methods as effective as this that can teach teens how to listen, be patient, and find the best way to approach a difficult situation. (6) These are real-life skills that they need for college and to become well-informed, conscientious adults.
(7) In fact, creating independent thinkers should be the goal of all educational programs, whether they are implemented in or outside of an academic environment.

23. What is the main point (conclusion) of the argument?
   a. sentence 1
   b. sentence 2
   c. sentence 3
   d. sentence 4

24. Which of the following is the strongest support for the conclusion?
   a. sentence 2
   b. sentence 4
   c. sentence 5
   d. sentence 7

25. Sentence 5 is which of the following?
   a. It is reasonable evidence based on a statistic.
   b. It is reasonable evidence based on common sense.
   c. It is based on personal experience.
   d. It is not reasonable evidence.

Read the following passages carefully and answer the questions that follow.

Roberta lost ten pounds in February. That month, she put in a great deal of overtime at work. She had also been trying to save money to take a few courses at the community college in the summer. In addition, she had been getting off the bus a mile away from work so that she'd get exercise each day.

26. Which of the following is most likely the *primary reason* for Roberta's weight loss?
   a. She was under too much stress from working so much.
   b. She forgot to eat because she was working so much.
   c. She was trying to save money by not spending it on food.
   d. She was getting exercise each day by walking a mile to work.

27. Based on the passage, which of the following can we logically conclude?
   a. Roberta planned on losing ten pounds in February.
   b. It was a coincidence that Roberta lost ten pounds after she began increasing her exercise.
   c. Roberta thought that working overtime would help her lose weight.
   d. Roberta was trying to lose ten pounds by the summer.

28. A young man is walking down the street when he sees that a pile of burning leaves has gotten out of control and the fire is about to spread to the adjacent house. Which of the following should he do first?
   a. Run down the street looking for a phone.
   b. Attempt to put out the fire.
   c. Warn the inhabitants of the house.
   d. Move a safe distance away from the fire.

Ellen is in charge of the annual holiday party for ABC Company. She wants everyone to be happy with the location, so she decides to take a survey. There are 80 employees; 20 are in management, 40 are sales representatives, and 20 are support staff.

29. If Ellen surveys ten employees, her survey results are
   a. *very likely* to accurately reflect the sentiments of all of the employees.
   b. *likely* to accurately reflect the sentiments of all of the employees.
   c. *very unlikely* to accurately reflect the sentiments of all of the employees.

30. If Ellen surveys 20 employees who are all members of management, her survey results are
   a. *very likely* to accurately reflect the sentiments of all of the employees.
   b. *likely* to accurately reflect the sentiments of all of the employees.
   c. *very unlikely* to accurately reflect the sentiments of all of the employees.

31. Ellen would get the most accurate results by surveying
   a. ten managers, 20 salespeople, and five support staff.
   b. ten managers, 20 salespeople, and ten support staff.
   c. 20 managers, 20 salespeople, and 20 support staff.
   d. ten managers, ten salespeople, and ten support staff.

32. Every time you play your stereo loudly, you notice that your upstairs neighbor puts on her stereo loudly, too. When you turn yours down, she turns hers back down. You therefore conclude
   a. your neighbor likes to play her music at the same time you play yours.
   b. your neighbor likes to play her music loudly, too.
   c. your neighbor is just showing off her stereo system.
   d. your neighbor has to turn up her stereo to drown out yours.

33. Beverly is putting together the schedule for her new employees. Each employee has to work two days a week. Andrew (A) can only work on Mondays, Wednesdays, and Fridays. Brenda (B) can only work on Mondays, Tuesdays, and Wednesdays. Carla (C) can only work on Tuesdays and Fridays. David (D) can work any day except Wednesdays, and Edward (E) can only work on Thursdays and Fridays. Which of the following is the best schedule?

	Monday	Tuesday	Wednesday	Thursday	Friday
a.	B & D	A & D	A & B	C & E	C & E
b.	A & D	B & C	A & B	D & E	C & E
c.	B & C	C & D	A & D	B & E	A & E
d.	A & D	B & C	C & E	B & E	A & D

Use the following paragraph to answer questions 34 and 35.

Joe, Karl, Larry, and Mike all work for the same company. Joe has been there two years longer than Karl and one year less than Larry. Mike has been there one year longer than Karl. Larry has been there for ten years.

34. Who has been there the longest?
   a. Joe
   b. Karl
   c. Larry
   d. Mike

35. Who is the newest employee?
   a. Joe
   b. Karl
   c. Larry
   d. Mike

► Answer Key

You can find relevant instruction and examples for any item(s) you miss in the lesson(s) listed to the right of each correct answer.

1. **b.** Lesson 2
2. **c.** Lesson 2
3. **a.** Lesson 3
4. **c.** Lesson 3
5. **b.** Lesson 3
6. **b.** Lesson 6
7. **c.** Lesson 5
8. **a.** Lesson 11
9. **c.** Lesson 12
10. **a.** Lesson 13
11. **b.** Lesson 11
12. **c.** Lesson 11
13. **c.** Lesson 14
14. **b.** Lesson 16
15. **a.** Lesson 16
16. **d.** Lessons 7–9
17. **b.** Lesson 11
18. **c.** Lesson 6
19. **a.** Lesson 13
20. **b.** Lesson 17

21. **d.** Lesson 4
22. **c.** Lesson 4
23. **a.** Lesson 7
24. **c.** Lessons 8, 9
25. **b.** Lesson 9
26. **d.** Lesson 17
27. **a.** Lesson 17
28. **c.** Lessons 2, 19
29. **c.** Lesson 18
30. **c.** Lesson 18
31. **b.** Lesson 18
32. **d.** Lesson 15
33. **b.** Lesson 19
34. **c.** Lessons 15, 19
35. **b.** Lessons 15, 19

Reasoning Skills Success
Lessons 1–20

1 ▶ Critical Thinking and Reasoning Skills

LESSON SUMMARY

You've probably heard the terms "critical thinking" and "reasoning skills" many times, in many different contexts. But what exactly does it mean to "think critically"? And just what are "reasoning skills"? This lesson will answer these questions and show you why critical thinking and reasoning skills are so important.

o matter who you are or what you do, you have to make decisions on a regular basis. You may not realize it, but even those decisions that seem like second nature—like deciding what to wear when you're getting dressed in the morning—require some critical thinking and reasoning skills. When you decide what to wear, you take many factors into consideration—the weather forecast; the current temperature; your plans for the day (where are you going? who will you see?); your comfort level (will you be walking a lot? sitting all day?); and so on. Thus, you are already a critical thinker on some level. But your life is complicated, and you face decisions that are much more difficult than choosing what to wear. How do you handle a conflict? Solve a problem? Resolve a crisis? Make a moral or ethical decision?

> "The person who thinks before he acts seldom has to apologize for his acts."
>
> —Napoleon Hill
> *(Think and Grow Rich)*

While there's no guarantee you'll always make the right decision or find the most effective solution to a problem, there *is* a way to significantly improve your odds—and that is by improving your critical thinking and reasoning skills.

▶ What Are Critical Thinking and Reasoning Skills?

To improve your critical thinking and reasoning skills, you need to know exactly what they are.

Critical Thinking

Think for a minute about the words *critical thinking*. What does this phrase mean? Essentially, **critical thinking** is a decision-making process. Specifically, critical thinking means carefully considering a problem, claim, question, or situation in order to determine the best solution. That is, when you think critically, you take the time to consider all sides of an issue, evaluate evidence, and imagine different scenarios and possible outcomes. It sounds like a lot of work, but the same basic critical thinking skills can be applied to all types of situations.

Critical thinking is so important because it helps you determine:

- How to best solve a problem
- Whether to accept or reject a claim
- How to best answer a question
- How to best handle a situation

Reasoning Skills

Reasoning skills, on the other hand, deal more with the *process* of getting from point A, the problem, to point B, the solution. You can get there haphazardly, or you can get there by reason.

A **reason** is a motive or cause for something—a justification for thoughts, actions, or opinions. In other words, it's *why* you do, say, or think what you do. But your reasons for doing things aren't always reasonable—as you know if you've ever done or said something in the heat of the moment. **Reasoning skills** ask you to use good sense and base your reasons on facts, evidence, or logical conclusions rather than just on your emotions. In short, when you decide on the best way to handle a situation or determine the best solution to a problem, you should have *logical* (rather than purely *emotional*) reasons for coming to that conclusion.

Logical: according to reason; according to conclusions drawn from evidence or good common sense
Emotional: drawn from emotions, from intense mental feelings

► The Difference between Reason and Emotion

It would be false to say that anything emotional is not reasonable. In fact, it's perfectly valid to take your emotions into consideration when you make decisions. After all, how you feel is very important. But if there's *no* logic or reason behind your decisions, you're usually in for trouble.

Let's say, for example, that you need to buy a car. This is a rather big decision, so it's important that you make it wisely. You'll want to be sure that you:

- Carefully consider your options
- Consider different possibilities and outcomes
- Have logical reasons to support your final decision

It may seem obvious that you need to choose a car that best suits your lifestyle and your budget. For example, as much as you might like sports cars, you shouldn't buy the new special edition Corvette if you have four children and a tight budget. But for a variety of emotional reasons, many people *do* make these kinds of unwise, unreasonable decisions. They may have thought critically and still made the wrong choice because they let their emotions override their sense of logic and reason.

Practice

1. For practice, imagine this scenario—buying a new car—and apply critical thinking and reasoning skills to it. First, critical thinking: What different things should you take into consideration when thinking about what kind of car to buy? List at least five different considerations. One is already listed for you.

Things to consider:
1. price
2. size
3. milage
4. Age of car
5. condition

Answers

You probably listed several important issues, such as:

- Size and style of the car: two-door vs. four-door, roomy vs. sporty
- Gas mileage
- Condition: new or used
- Safety features
- Amenities: stereo, air conditioning, and so on
- Overall reliability and quality
- Manufacturer
- Comfort level: leg room, type of seats, and so on
- Warranty
- Looks: color, shape, design

► Justifying Your Decision

One way to help ensure that you're using your critical thinking and reasoning skills is to always justify your decisions and actions. Why did you do what you did? Why did you make that decision? Why did that seem like the best solution? Try this with even your most everyday decisions and actions. You'll get to know your current decision-making process, and you'll be able to determine where in that process you can become more effective.

Practice

2. Imagine that you really do have to buy a car. Using your critical thinking and reasoning skills, write down what kind of car (model, new or used, etc.) you'd buy and why. You can make up the specifics; what's important is that you include several different reasons that show you've thought about your decision carefully and critically.

Kind of car:

Approximate price:

Reasons for this choice:

Answers

Answers will vary. Here's a sample answer.

Kind of car: 1994 Toyota Camry
Approximate price: $6,000
Reasons for this choice:
- Excellent condition for a used car—recently inspected; new tires
- Only 3,500 miles on the car
- Good gas mileage—30 miles per gallon
- Affordable—just within my budget
- Good safety features
- Big trunk, which I need to deliver equipment and supplies
- Decent stereo and air conditioning included
- Red—my favorite color

▶ Why Critical Thinking and Reasoning Skills Are Important

You will face (if you don't already) situations on the job, at home, and at school that require critical thinking and reasoning skills. By improving these skills, you can improve your success in everything you do. Specifically, strong critical thinking and reasoning skills will help you:

- Compose and support strong, logical arguments
- Assess the validity of other people's arguments
- Make more effective and logical decisions
- Solve problems more efficiently

Essentially, these four skills make up **problem-solving skills**. For example, if someone wants to change your mind and convince you of something, you have a "problem"—you have to decide whether or not to change your beliefs, whether to accept that person's argument. Similarly, when you have a choice to make, or a position you'd like to support, you have a different type of "problem" to solve—what choice to make, how to support your position. Thus, this book will use the term *problem solving* to refer to any one of these situations. Problem solving will be the focus of the next lesson.

Practice

Use your critical thinking and reasoning skills to solve the following problem.

Jorge has been offered a promotion with United Casualty, where he has worked for five years. He has also been offered a similar job by the company's main competitor, The Harrison Group. Harrison is willing to pay Jorge a little more for a comparable position. What should Jorge do?

3. List the different issues Jorge should consider in making this difficult decision.

4. Make a decision for Jorge and explain why that's a good decision for him. Feel free to make up the various circumstances in his life—for example, whether Jorge lives closer to United or to Harrison. The more reasons you can give for his decision, the better.

Answers

3. Some of the issues Jorge needs to consider include:

- Money
- Job security
- Benefits
- Compatibility with coworkers
- Job environment
- Specific job duties
- Location/commute
- Hours
- Room for advancement
- Stability of company

4. Answers will vary. Here's a sample answer:

Jorge should stay with United Casualty. It's a much shorter commute—half the time it would take to get to Harrison—so he would save both time and gas money, as well as reduce wear and tear on his car. Currently, he has an excellent relationship with his supervisors at United and enjoys working with his coworkers. United is a solid, stable company—it's been in business for over 40 years and had a record year last year. Harrison, on the other hand, is only ten years old and has recently had a great deal of employee turnover.

▶ In Short

Critical thinking is the act of carefully considering a problem, claim, question, or situation in order to determine the best "solution." Reasoning skills, which go hand-in-hand with critical thinking, ask you to base your decisions on facts, evidence, or logical conclusions. Critical thinking and reasoning skills are implemented simultaneously to help you make smarter decisions and solve problems effectively. They also help you make stronger arguments and better evaluate the arguments of others.

Skill Building until Next Time

Notice how many decisions you make throughout the day and how many different problems you face. What kind of decisions and problems do you encounter most often at home? At work? At school?

- Write down the process you went through to make a decision or solve a problem today. What did you do to get from point A, the problem, to point B, the solution?
- Evaluate a decision or problem you solved recently. Do you think it was a wise decision or effective solution? Why or why not? Did you consider the range of issues, or did you neglect to take certain issues into consideration? Did you make your decision based mostly on reason or mostly on your emotions?

2 ▶ Problem-Solving Strategies

LESSON SUMMARY

You face problems every day, and sometimes they can be overwhelming. In this lesson, you'll learn how to pinpoint the main issue of a problem and how to break it down into its various parts, thus making the problem more manageable.

nd we will show, beyond a reasonable doubt, that my client is not guilty of committing the heinous act he is accused of." If you've ever watched a legal drama or sat on a jury yourself, this statement should sound familiar. You probably know that sometimes jury members are faced with very serious dilemmas. In fact, many times, the fate of a defendant rests in their final decision, or *verdict*.

Luckily, not all situations or problems are as formidable as deciding the destiny of another human being. But everyone faces his or her share of problems, and it's important to handle them quickly and effectively. Critical thinking and reasoning skills can help you do just that.

▶ Definition: What Is a Problem?

Let's begin by defining the word *problem*. In terms of critical thinking and reasoning skills, a **problem** is any situation or matter that is challenging to solve, thus requiring you to make a difficult decision. That decision can be about anything—how to answer a perplexing question, how to handle a complicated situation, how to convince someone to see your point of view, or even how to solve a puzzle or mystery. For example, you might face the following kinds of problems:

Questions: Should a U.S. presidential term be more than four years? Should you report your coworker for stealing?

Situations: Your friends are pressuring you to go to a party tonight, but you promised your brother you'd help him on a project. What do you do?

Convincing: How do you convince Joe that he shouldn't treat his girlfriend so poorly?

Solving: Who stole the money from the safe? How can you make enough money to pay for college?

▶ Identifying the Problem

The first step to solving any problem is to *identify* the problem. This may sound obvious—of course you need to know what the problem is. But it's important to take this step, because in real life, with all its complications, it's easy to lose sight of the real problem at hand. When this happens, the problem becomes much more complicated than it needs to be because you end up focusing on secondary issues rather than what's really at stake.

Once you've identified the problem, you need to break it down into its parts. This is an essential step because it gives you a sense of the **scope** of the problem. How big is it? How many issues are there? Sometimes, at first glance, problems seem so big that a solution seems impossible. Other times, you may underestimate the size of a problem and end up making a poor decision because you overlook an important factor. By

breaking a problem down into its parts, you may find it's not as big a problem as you thought—or that it's much more complicated than you initially anticipated. Either way, when you break a problem down, you make it manageable—big or small, you can take it on one issue at a time.

Practice

To see exactly how breaking down a problem works, read the following scenario:

Your car has broken down and will have to be in the shop for two or three days. It's Monday, and you need to get to work, which is 20 miles north of where you live. The nearest bus stop is ten miles away to the east. Your brother, who lives near you, works 20 miles to the south. The nearest cab company is 20 miles to the west.

1. Which of the following best expresses the real issue or problem?
   a. how you will be able to afford the repairs
   b. how you can convince your brother to give you a ride
   c. how you are going to get to work
   d. whether you will be able to afford a cab

Answer

The answer is **c**—how you are going to get to work. This is the main problem you must solve—the "big picture."

Notice, however, that each of the other answers above is a *sub*issue; each option except choice **c** is a *specific* way to address the larger, more general problem. It's important to remember that choices **a, b,** and **d** are just *parts* of the problem. Also, there may be other parts that are not listed here. If one of those options doesn't work out, other viable options remain.

Practice

Here's another scenario:

> You're the leader of a small production-line team. Two members of the team have had a serious fight. The other two team members witnessed the fight. Everyone seems to have a different story.

2. Which of the following best expresses the real issue or problem?
   a. who started the fight
   b. what really happened
   c. whose version of what happened you should believe
   d. how to get the team working together again
   e. how to prevent future disputes

Answer

This situation is a bit more complicated than the first. To get the best answer, you need to ask yourself where the real issue lies, what's really at stake. Is it more important to determine what happened, or to decide how to fix what happened?

It's very easy to get caught up in the details of the fight, trying to find out who's to blame. But while that's important, the real problem is to figure out how to keep making progress, and how to get the team working together again, which is reflected in choice **d.** The other choices, except choice **e**, illustrate different components of that larger problem.

In order to solve this problem, you *do* need to address both issues in choices **a** and **b:** who started it and what really happened. And in order to do that, you'll need to take into consideration choice **c** as well: whose version of what happened you should believe. Furthermore, you should also keep choice **e** in mind so that you can minimize this type of problem in the future.

▶ Breaking the Problem into Its Parts

Now that you've identified the main problem, it's time to identify the various parts of that problem. You already know several issues:

Problem: How to get the team working together again

Parts of the problem:
- Who started the fight
- What really happened
- Whose version of what happened you should believe
- How to prevent future disputes

Practice

3. Each of these issues must be addressed in order to solve the problem. But these aren't the only issues. Can you think of any other parts of this problem? Write them here:

   ■

   ■

   ■

   ■

Answers

You might have added several issues, such as:

Parts of the problem:
- Who started the fight
- What really happened
- Whose version of what happened you should believe
- How to prevent future disputes
- How to reprimand the members who were fighting
- Whether or not to report the fight to your superiors
- How to exercise your authority
- How to carry out your investigation

If you thought of any other issues, add them here.
-
-

▶ Prioritizing Issues

The next step is to decide how to tackle the issues above. Clearly, some are more important than others, and some must be addressed before others. That's why it's essential to rank the parts of the problem in the order in which you think they should be addressed. Which issues need to be dealt with first? Second? Third? Are there some issues that must be solved before you can deal with others?

Practice
4. Use your critical thinking and reasoning skills to prioritize the previously mentioned issues.

Answer

Answers will vary, depending upon what other issues you identified. Here's how the previous list might be prioritized:

Parts of the problem, in order of importance:
- How to exercise your authority
- How to carry out your investigation
- Who started the fight
- What really happened
- Whose version of what happened you should believe
- How to reprimand the members who were fighting
- Whether or not to report the fight to your superiors
- How to prevent future disputes

▶ Relevance of Issues

When you're breaking down a problem, it's important that you make sure your issues are relevant to the problem. That is, each issue should be clearly related to the matter at hand. It's often obvious when something isn't relevant. Whether you like your pizza plain or with pepperoni, for example, clearly has nothing to do with this problem. But something like who has been on the job longer might be relevant. It depends upon what the fight was about.

One thing to keep in mind, however, is that personal preferences are often brought in as issues when they shouldn't be. For example, you may like certain members of your production team better than others, but that doesn't mean that these people are more believable than the others. In other words, your friendship with one or the other, or lack thereof, should not be relevant to the situation. Lesson 8 has more to say about this kind of bias.

Practice

Read the following scenario carefully and then answer the questions that follow.

You just inherited a large amount of money from your great uncle. In his will, however, he specified that you must invest that money for ten years before you can withdraw any cash. Your spouse says you should invest in the stock market. Your father says the stock market is too risky, that you should put the money right in the bank. Your friend says put the money in mutual funds—they're less risky than the market but give you a better return than the bank.

5. The main problem or issue is
   a. whether or not stocks are too risky.
   b. whether putting the money in the bank gives high enough return.
   c. whose advice you should take.
   d. how you should invest the money.

6. What are the parts of the problem?

   -
   -
   -
   -
   -

7. In what order should you address the parts of the problem?

   -
   -
   -
   -
   -

Answers

5. The main problem is choice **d,** how you should invest the money.

6. You may have broken the problem down into the following parts:
   - How can I find out about these options?
   - What are the different options for investing?
   - What does my spouse think?
   - What kind of investment gives me the most return?
   - What kind of investment gives me the most security?
   - What's more important to me—return or security?
   - Whose opinion should I trust?

7. You should probably address the parts of the problem in the following order:
   - What's more important to me, return or security?
   - What does my spouse think?
   - What are the different options for investing?
   - How can I find out about these options?
   - Whose opinion should I trust?
   - What kind of investment gives me the most return?
   - What kind of investment gives me the most security?

► In Short

A **problem** is any situation or matter that is challenging to solve, thus requiring you to make a difficult decision. Breaking problems down can help you make even big problems manageable. The first step to effective problem solving is to clearly identify the main problem. Then, break the problem down into its various parts. After you rank the parts in order of priority, check to make sure each issue is relevant.

Skill Building until Next Time

- Take a problem that you come across today and break it down. Identify the main issue and each of its parts. Then, prioritize the parts.
- While sitcoms often drastically simplify the problems we face in real life, dramas like *Law and Order* and *ER* often show characters dealing with complex problems. Watch one of these shows and notice how the characters work through their problems. Do they correctly identify the real problem? Do they break it down into its parts? Evaluate their problem-solving strategies.

3 ▶ Thinking vs. Knowing

LESSON SUMMARY

One of the keys to effective critical thinking and reasoning skills is the ability to distinguish between fact and opinion. This lesson will show you the difference—and why it matters.

I f you've ever watched the popular TV series *CSI,* you know that the investigators on the show rely heavily on *evidence* to prove their theories and solve their cases. What does this mean? It means that before they point any fingers, they use scientific proof to justify their claims.

As a viewer, you may have an *opinion* as to who committed the crime in question—that is, you may *believe* one character over another. But according to the crime scene investigators, who did what and when is a matter of *fact.* That is, with enough evidence, they don't believe—they know—because they can *prove* it.

▶ Definition: Fact vs. Opinion

Before we go any further, let's define *fact* and *opinion*.

Facts are:
- Things *known* for certain to have happened
- Things *known* for certain to be true
- Things *known* for certain to exist

Opinions, on the other hand, are:

- Things *believed* to have happened
- Things *believed* to be true
- Things *believed* to exist

Essentially, the difference between fact and opinion is the difference between *believing* and *knowing*. Opinions may be *based* on facts, but they are still what we *think*, not what we *know*. Opinions are debatable; facts usually are not. A good test for whether something is a fact or opinion is to ask yourself, "Can this statement be debated? Is this known for certain to be true?" If you can answer *yes* to the first question, you have an opinion; if you answer *yes* to the second, you have a fact. If you're not sure, then it's best to assume that it's an opinion until you can *verify* that it is indeed a fact.

Fact: based on what is **known**

Opinion: based on what is **believed**

▶ Why the Difference between Fact and Opinion Is Important

When you're making decisions, it's important to be able to distinguish between fact and opinion—between what you or others *believe* and what you or others *know* to be true. When you make decisions, assess others' arguments, and support your own arguments, use facts, as they generally carry more weight than opinions. For example, if I try to convince my boss that I deserve a raise and I use facts to support my argument, I'm much more likely to get that raise than if I simply use the opinion, "I think I deserve one." Notice the difference between the following two examples:

- "I really think I should get a raise. It's about time, and I deserve it. I've earned it."
- "I really think I deserve a raise. I've met all of my production goals since I've been here, my evaluations have been excellent, and I was employee of the month."

Notice in the second example, facts support the opinion that "I deserve a raise."

Furthermore, distinguishing between fact and opinion is important because people will often present their opinions as fact. When you're trying to make big decisions or solve complex problems, you need to know that you're working with evidence rather than emotions.

Practice

Read the following statements carefully. Which of the following are facts? Opinions? Write an **F** in the blank if the statement is a fact and an **O** if it is an opinion.

_____ **1.** People who have been out of school and in the workforce for several years make better students.

_____ **2.** More people than ever before are working for a few years before they go to college.

_____ **3.** Many companies provide tuition reimbursement for adults returning to school for college degrees.

_____ **4.** Most companies don't provide enough tuition reimbursement for their employees.

_____ **5.** At Hornig Steelworks, you won't get reimbursed unless you earn at least a C in any course you take.

Answers

1. O
2. F
3. F
4. O
5. F

Practice

To strengthen your ability to distinguish between fact and opinion, try turning a fact into an opinion. Here's a fact:

Americans pay federal, state, and local taxes.

An opinion is something debatable. Here are two opinions based on this fact:

Americans pay too much in taxes.

Americans should pay taxes only if they make over $40,000.

Now you try it.

6. Fact: Some states have raised their speed limits to 65 or more on major highways.
Opinion:

7. Fact: You can vote and go to war at age 18, but you can't legally drink alcohol until you're 21.
Opinion:

8. Fact: E-mail and other technologies are making it possible for more people to work from home than ever before.
Opinion:

9. Fact: Most college students are required to take some liberal arts *and* science courses, no matter what their majors.
Opinion:

Answers

Answers will vary. Here are sample answers:

6. States that have raised their speed limits to over 65 are playing with fire.
7. You should be allowed to drink at the same age you are eligible to go to war.
8. E-mail and other technologies are great because they enable us to work from home.
9. Most colleges should require students to take both liberal arts and science courses.

▶ Tentative Truths

Try this exercise. Label the following as either fact (**F**) or opinion (**O**).

_____**10.** I believe that the government has evidence of contact with aliens hidden in Roswell, New Mexico.

_____**11.** The government has evidence of contact with aliens hidden in Roswell, New Mexico.

You didn't by chance mark the first claim as **O** and the second claim as **F**, did you? If you did, it's easy to see why. The first claim is *presented* as an opinion ("I believe"), and it is therefore clearly an opinion. The second claim, however, is presented as a fact. But is it true? Is it something *known* for sure? Well, it can't really be proven or disproved, unless you have access to secret government documents. Statement 11 is what is called a **tentative truth**, since it is neither a fact nor an opinion. Until the truth of that matter can be verified—especially a matter that has been so controversial for so many years—it's best to hold on to a healthy measure of doubt.

Tentative truths need not deal with conspiracy theories or other issues of major importance. They can deal with issues as simple as this:

Volvos get 30 miles per gallon.

This is a matter of fact, and it sounds like something that should be accepted as true, but unless you got in a Volvo and drove around, you may not be able to verify it. You can *tentatively* accept it as fact, especially if the source is credible. **Credibility** is the key determinant of whether you should accept facts you can't verify yourself. The next lesson shows you how to determine credibility.

Practice

Determine whether the following claims are facts (F), opinions (O), or claims that you should accept as tentative truths (TT):

12. The country is divided into several time zones.

13. The time difference between New York City and Denver is three hours.

14. It's confusing to have so many different time zones.

Answers
12. F
13. **TT,** unless you happen to know the time difference, in which case you could call this a fact. In reality, this is a *false* fact; the difference between New York City and Denver is two hours.
14. O

▶ Fact vs. Opinion in Critical Reasoning

Now let's look at a situation where you have to use your critical thinking and reasoning skills to make a decision and where it will be important to distinguish between fact and opinion. Let's return to the example where you must invest your inheritance from your great uncle. In order to make a good decision, you need to know the difference between fact and opinion. You also have to be able to recognize when opinions are based on facts. First, let's continue to practice noticing the distinction between fact and opinion.

Practice
15. Read the following paragraphs carefully. **Highlight** the facts and underline the opinions.

Paragraph A:

There are lots of different ways to invest your money. Many people invest in stocks and bonds, but I think good old-fashioned savings accounts and CDs (certificates of deposit) are the best way to invest your hard-earned money. Stocks and bonds are often risky, and it doesn't make sense to gamble with your hard-earned money. True, regular savings accounts and CDs can't make you a millionaire overnight or provide the high returns some stock investments do. But unless you're an expert, it's hard to know which stocks will provide you with that kind of return. Besides, savings accounts and CDs are fully insured and provide steady, secure interest on your money. That makes a whole lot of cents.

Paragraph B:

Many folks are scared of the stock market—but they shouldn't be. True, the stock market is risky, but the gamble is worth it. Besides, playing it safe requires too much patience. The stock market is by far the best option for today's investors.

Answers

How did you do? Was it easy to distinguish between fact and opinion? Here's what your marked-up passages should look like:

Paragraph A

There are lots of different ways to invest your money. Many people invest in stocks and bonds, but <u>I think good old-fashioned savings accounts and CDs (certificates of deposit) are the best way to invest your hard-earned money.</u> **Stocks and bonds are often risky,** and <u>it doesn't make sense to gamble with your hard-earned money.</u> **True, regular savings accounts and CDs can't make you a millionaire overnight or provide the high returns some stock investments do.** <u>But unless you're an expert, it's hard to know which stocks will provide you with that kind of return.</u> Besides, **savings accounts and CDs are fully insured and provide steady, secure interest on your money.** <u>That makes a whole lot of cents.</u>

Paragraph B

Many folks are scared of the stock market—but <u>they shouldn't be.</u> **True, the stock market is risky,** but <u>the gamble is worth it.</u> Besides, <u>playing it safe requires too much patience.</u> <u>The stock market is by far the best option for today's investors.</u>

Practice

16. Now that you've distinguished fact from opinion in these paragraphs, which paragraph should you take more seriously when deciding what to do with your uncle's inheritance? Write your answer on a separate piece of paper.

Answer

You should have chosen **paragraph A** as the paragraph to take more seriously. Paragraph A has a good balance of fact and opinion; most of the writer's opinions are supported by facts. Paragraph B, on the other hand, includes several unsupported opinions.

▶ In Short

Distinguishing between fact and opinion is a vital critical thinking and reasoning skill. To make wise decisions and solve problems effectively, you need to know the difference between what people *think* (opinion) and what people *know* (fact); between what people *believe* to be true (opinion) and what *has been proven* to be true (fact). You should also be able to determine whether something presented as fact is really true or if you should accept it as a tentative truth.

Skill Building until Next Time

- Listen carefully to what people say today and try to determine whether they are stating a fact or expressing an opinion. If you're not sure, is it OK to accept it as a tentative truth?
- As you come across facts and opinions today, practice turning them into their opposites: Make facts out of opinions and opinions out of facts.

Who Makes the Claim?

LESSON SUMMARY

When we're faced with opinions and tentative truths, it's important to know how much we can trust our sources and how much they know about the subject at hand. This lesson will teach you how to evaluate the credibility of your sources so that you can make well-informed decisions.

You've decided you'd like to see a movie tonight, but you're not sure what to see. You're thinking about catching the latest Steven Spielberg movie, so you decide to find out what others think of it. Your coworker, who goes to the movies at least twice a week, says it's one of the best films he's ever seen, that you'll love it. Your sister, a legal secretary who knows you very well, says she thought it was OK, but she thinks you'll hate it. A review in the *Times* calls it "dull" and "uninspired," a "real disappointment." The full-page ad in the *Times*, however, calls it "dazzling," a "true cinematic triumph," and gives it "two thumbs up." So, do you go to see the movie or not?

In this instance, you're faced with many opinions—what various people *think* about the movie. So whose opinion should you value the most here? How do you make your decision?

▶ Definition: What Is Credibility?

When you're faced with a variety of opinions, one of the most important things to consider is the **credibility** of those giving their opinion. That is, you need to consider whose opinion is the most trustworthy and valid in the particular situation.

> **Credibility:** believability; trustworthiness

Credibility also plays a very important role when dealing with those tentative truths you encountered in the last lesson. Whenever you're offered opinions or facts that you aren't comfortable accepting and aren't able to verify, the credibility of your source is crucial in helping you decide whether or not to accept these opinions or tentative truths.

▶ How to Determine Credibility

Several factors determine the credibility of a source. One is your previous experience with that source. Do you have any reason to doubt the truthfulness or reliability of this source based on past experience?

Next, you need to consider your source's potential for bias as well as level of expertise. But let's return to our opening scenario for a moment. In this situation, we have four different opinions to consider:

- What your coworker thinks
- What your sister thinks
- What the *Times* review says
- What the *Times* ad says

Of the four, which is probably the *least* credible (least trustworthy) source, and why?

You should have chosen the *Times* advertisement as the least credible source. Why? Simply because it is an ad, and no advertisement is going to say anything bad about the product it's trying to sell, is it? Advertisements generally have limited credibility because they're *biased*.

▶ Recognizing Bias

A **bias** is an opinion or feeling that strongly favors one side over others; a predisposition to support one side; or a prejudice against other sides. The full-page ad in the *Times* clearly has a vested interest in supporting the movie. No matter how good or how bad it really is, the ad is going to print only favorable comments so that you will go see the film.

Advertising has a clear money-making agenda. But bias is prevalent in everyday situations, too. For example, you may be less likely to believe what your neighbor has to say about candidate Warren simply because your neighbor keeps thoughtlessly starting construction on the new addition to his house at 6 A.M. In that case, you'd be influenced by your annoyance with your neighbor rather than the validity of his opinion. You need to remember to separate your feelings about your neighbor from what he actually has to say.

Similarly, another neighbor may have great things to say about candidate Warren, but if you know that this neighbor is Warren's cousin, or that Warren has promised your neighbor a seat on the local council, then you can see that your neighbor has something at stake in getting you to vote for Warren. It's important, therefore, to know as much as possible about your sources when deciding how heavily to weigh their opinions.

Practice

Read the following scenario. Write **B** next to anyone whom you think might be biased. If you think the person is likely to have an unbiased, reasonable opinion, write **U** in the blank.

Scenario: Congress is currently debating a tax reform proposal that makes filing taxes easier.

_____ **1.** The author of the proposal

_____ **2.** A professor of tax law

_____ **3.** A tax preparer

_____ **4.** The average taxpayer

Answers

1-B; 2-U; 3-B; 4-U. The author of the proposal (1) has a vested interest in the proposal and in seeing that it is passed. A tax preparer (3), meanwhile, has a vested interest in the proposal being rejected, because if the reform makes filing taxes easier, he just might lose business. The professor (2) may have a definite opinion about the proposal, but chances are she's pretty objective—she doesn't win or lose by having the proposal passed or rejected (except, of course, as a taxpayer herself). And the average taxpayer (4) will probably like the proposal and for good reason, but not because of any bias.

Level of Expertise

Return now to the opening example about the movie. You're down to three possible choices. How do you determine whose opinion is most credible? It's not going to be easy, but let's provide some additional criteria for determining credibility. Once you identify any possible biases, you need to carefully consider the next criteria: **expertise**.

Generally speaking, the more a person knows about a subject—the more expertise he or she has in that area—the more comfortable you should feel accepting his or her opinion. That is, in general, the greater the expertise, the greater the credibility.

In this situation, expertise falls into two categories: knowledge of movies and knowledge of you and your personal tastes. So you need to consider how much these three sources know both about what makes a good movie _and_ how much these three sources know about what you enjoy in a film.

Practice

Rank each of these three sources in each area of expertise. Use 1 for the source with the most expertise and 3 for the source with the least.

5. Knowledge of movies:
_____coworker
_____sister
_____Times_ review

6. Knowledge of you and your taste in movies:
_____coworker
_____sister
_____Times_ review

Answers

5. Knowledge of movies: 1–*Times* review; 2–coworker; and 3–sister. Even though your coworker may not be a professional movie critic like the writer of the *Times* review, he goes to see enough movies to have developed some expertise. You may not agree with his criteria for determining what makes a good movie, but at least he should be granted some credibility.

6. Knowledge of you and your taste in movies: Probably 1–sister; 2–coworker; and 3–*Times* review, though this order can vary greatly, depending on the situation. Where you rank the *Times* review depends entirely upon your past experience with the *Times*. If you've never read a *Times* review before or you don't usually, then it should probably be ranked as the lowest in expertise here. However, if you regularly read the reviews, you may have found that you generally agree with the opinions of the reviewer—that is, you usually like the movies that get good reviews and dislike the movies that get poor ones. In this case, you can rank the *Times* review first. On the other hand, you may have found that you generally disagree with the reviewers—that you usually like the movies that they don't. In that case, the *Times* review would be the lowest on your list.

Determining Level of Expertise

In many a courtroom, lawyers will call an "expert witness" to the stand to support their case. For example, in a murder case where the defendant is pleading insanity, the prosecution and the defense might call upon psychologists who can provide expert opinions about the defendant's ability to distinguish between right and wrong. These expert witnesses are usually outside the case—that is, they are usually not involved in the alleged crime and usually do not have any relationship to or with the defendant; otherwise, they might be biased.

For this testimony to be helpful to either side, however, the jury must be convinced that the expert witness is indeed an *expert*; they must be assured of his or her credibility. The lawyers will help establish the witness's credibility by pointing out one or more of the following credentials:

- Education
- Experience
- Job or position
- Reputation
- Achievements

These five criteria are what you should examine when determining someone's level of expertise and therefore credibility. One category is not necessarily more important than the other, though generally a person's education and experience carry the most weight.

An outstanding expert witness at this trial, therefore, might have the following profile:

Dr. Joanne Francis

Education: PhD, Harvard University

Experience: Ten years at County Medical Hospital; 15 years at Harvard Psychiatric Center

Position: Chief of Psychiatric Care at Harvard Psychiatric Center; teaches graduate courses at Harvard

Reputation: Ranked one of the ten best on the East Coast

Accomplishments: Has won several awards; was asked to serve on a federal judicial committee to establish guidelines for determining insanity; has written three textbooks and published 20 journal articles

Notice how strong Dr. Francis is in each of the five categories.

Practice

Using the criteria to determine expertise, rank the choices **a–d** for credibility. Use 1 for the source with most expertise and 4 for the source with the least.

7. How to invest your inheritance from your great uncle
   a. your great uncle's financial advisor
   b. an investment banker
   c. your favorite bank teller
   d. *Investors Weekly* magazine

8. What kind of car you should buy
   a. your brother
   b. your mechanic
   c. *Consumer Reports*
   d. the car dealer nearest you

Answers

7. **1–d; 2–a; 3–b; 4–c,** though it's a close call between 2 and 3. Here, *Investors Weekly* is ranked first because it is the least biased and probably most comprehensive source. Your great uncle's financial advisor, however, also has a very high level of expertise. Clearly he's done a good job, since you received a substantial inheritance from your great uncle; he obviously believes in investing. The only reason the advisor is ranked second is the potential for bias: He may want to have you as his client. That's also why the investment banker is ranked third. Though she may be quite knowledgeable, she, too, may have certain ideas and opinions specific to her business, and she probably wants you as a client. Also, because she's a banker, she may be more limited in her breadth of knowledge than a financial advisor. Finally, your favorite bank teller has several problems, the biggest being that her education and experience with investments are probably quite limited.

8. Your ranking here depends upon how much your brother knows about cars. If he has bought several cars in recent years, is the kind of guy who does research before making a purchase, and has a lifestyle and budget similar to yours, then his level of expertise will be pretty high. If your brother doesn't know much about cars, the sources should be ranked in the following order: **1–c; 2–b; 3–d.** The car dealer is the most biased of the sources, and the salespeople may not know a great deal about makes and models of cars besides those on their lot.

▶ Special Case: Eyewitness Credibility

One of the most difficult but important times to determine credibility is when there are eyewitnesses to a crime or other incident. Unfortunately, just because someone was at the scene doesn't mean his or her account is credible. One obvious factor that can interfere with witness credibility is bias. Let's say two coworkers, Andrea and Brady, get in a fight. There are three witnesses. Al is friends with Andrea; Bea is friends with Brady; and Cecil is friends with both Andrea and Brady. Chances are that what Al "saw" will favor Andrea and what Bea saw will favor Brady. What Cecil saw, however, will probably be closest to the unbiased truth.

Other factors can also interfere with witness credibility. If an incident occurs at a bar, for example, we have several possible interferences. It was probably dark, smoky, and noisy, and the witnesses may have been drinking, tired, or simply not paying very much attention to their surroundings.

In all eyewitness accounts, the longer the time between the event and the time of questioning, the more unreliable the account of the witness will most likely be. Think for a minute about your childhood. Did you ever tell a story about something that happened when you were little, only to be corrected by a parent or sibling who says, "That's not what happened"? Their version is different. Why? Because our memory fades quickly and can be influenced by our own ideas about ourselves and others.

Thus, there are at least four factors that influence the credibility of eyewitnesses:

1. Bias
2. Environment
3. Physical and emotional condition of the witness
4. Time between event and recollection of event

Practice

Imagine you are a police officer who has just arrived at the scene of a fight between two young men on a street corner. Three people witnessed the incident, which occurred at 9:00 P.M. You arrive and begin interviewing witnesses at 9:20 P.M. The street corner is well lit.

9. Who do you think is the most credible witness, and why?

Witness A is an elderly woman who was sitting on the stoop about ten feet from the corner. She was wearing her glasses, but she admits that she needs a stronger prescription. Her hearing, however, is fine. She doesn't know either boy involved in the incident, though she's seen them around the neighborhood before.

Witness B is a friend of one of the boys but does not know the other. He is an outstanding student at the local high school and a star basketball player. He was at the deli around the corner buying bread when he heard the boys shouting and came out to see what was going on. He had just had a fight with his girlfriend.

Witness C is a stranger to the neighborhood. He was crossing the street toward the corner when the boys started fighting. He has 20/20 vision. He is 45 and has two teenage children. He was only a few feet away from the boys when the fight occurred.

Answer

9. Though **Witness C** may have been distracted by traffic, chances are he's the most credible eyewitness. He was heading toward the corner and was looking at the boys. He may not have been able to hear what happened in the beginning, but he should have been able to see exactly what occurred. His vision is perfect and there's no reason to suspect any bias.

Witness A is probably next on the list. Though she may not have been able to see as clearly as **Witness C,** she was close enough to have heard what passed between the boys. Again, we have little reason to suspect bias.

Witness B is probably the least credible witness. Though he has a good reputation, he has two strikes against him. The first is that he is friends with one of the boys, so he may be biased. The second is that he had just had a fight with his girlfriend, so he may have been distracted and not paying much attention.

▶ In Short

When you're making decisions and solving problems, it's important to consider the credibility of your sources. To determine whether a source is trustworthy, you must first rule out the potential for bias and then evaluate the source's level of expertise. Expertise is determined by education, experience, job or position, reputation, and achievements. Eyewitness credibility, on the other hand, must take into consideration the witness's potential for bias, the environment, the condition of the witness, and the time lapse between the event and the witness's recollection of the event.

Skill Building until Next Time

- As you talk to others today and hear any of their opinions or tentative truths, think about their credibility. What biases might they have, if any? What is their level of expertise? Remember, a source's credibility can change depending upon the subject matter of the claim.
- Watch a detective or legal drama, like *Without a Trace, Judging Amy,* or *Law & Order.* As you watch, pay particular attention to how the detectives and lawyers determine the credibility of their witnesses and others involved in the case.

Partial Claims and Half-Truths

LESSON SUMMARY

Every day, we're bombarded with partial claims and half-truths aimed at getting us to buy a product or support a cause. This lesson will show you how to recognize incomplete claims and hidden agendas.

You're relaxing on your sofa watching your favorite television show when it's time for a commercial break. Suddenly, a handsome announcer comes on the screen and tells you that new Stain-Ex laundry detergent outperforms the leading brand *and* costs less! Sounds like a great product. But should you run out and buy it?

Well, besides the fact that you're probably quite comfortable on your couch, the answer is no—at least not yet. Not until you investigate further.

▶ The Trouble with Incomplete Claims

Why shouldn't you go out and buy Stain-Ex? After all, it "outperforms the leading brand" *and* "costs less!" So what's the problem?

The problem is that while the announcer's claims *sound* like facts, they're really quite misleading—and meant to be. Maybe Stain-Ex did "outperform" the leading brand (which brand is that?)—but in what category? Stain removing? Whitening? Brightening? Sudsing? Rinsing? Fragrance? The ad doesn't say. The claim *sounds* good, but because it is incomplete, you don't know exactly *what* it's claiming. And until you determine what it's claiming, it's difficult to accept it even as a tentative truth.

The commercial also claims that Stain-Ex "costs less." Because the first claim compares Stain-Ex to the leading brand, it's easy to assume that Stain-Ex costs less than the *leading brand*. But is that what the ad really says? If you aren't listening carefully, it's easy to hear what you want to hear, or rather, what the makers of Stain-Ex want you to hear. The commercial simply says that Stain-Ex "costs less." It never says less than *what*. To assume it costs less than the leading brand is to fall right into the ad's trap. This tactic is good for the makers of Stain-Ex, but not so good for you or the leading brand.

Flip through just about any popular magazine and you'll find page after page of advertisements that make this kind of incomplete claim. These ads may use vague words or phrases, leave out essential information, or compare incomparable items. For example, you might see an ad claiming that new Crispy Potato Chips have one-third the fat per serving of Munch Chips. Sounds good, right? But what important information has been left out? What do you need to know to determine whether this is a fair comparison?

What the ad leaves out is the serving size. Without that information, how do you know it's a fair comparison? Maybe a serving of Crispy Chips is two ounces, whereas a serving of Munch Chips is six ounces, in which case Crispy Chips is just as fattening as Munch Chips. To be on the safe side, beware of any comparison that is incomplete or vague.

Practice

Here are several incomplete claims and comparisons. Rewrite them so that they're complete.

Example:
Incomplete claim: Now with 20% more flavor!
Revised claim: Now with 20% more onion flavor than our old recipe!

1. Incomplete claim: Energy Batteries last longer!
Revised claim:

2. Incomplete claim: New and improved Mildew-Gone is tougher.
Revised claim:

3. Incomplete claim: Smooth-Touch toilet tissue—twice the paper at half the price!
Revised claim:

Answers

Answers will vary. Here are some possible revisions:

1. Energy Batteries last two hours longer than Forever Last!
2. New and improved Mildew-Gone is tougher on mildew stains than our old formula.
3. Smooth-Touch toilet tissue—twice as much paper as Thompson tissue at half the price per roll!

▶ Tests and Studies

The makers of the Stain-Ex commercial know you've become a savvy shopper, so they've remade their commercial. Now the announcer tells you:

> Studies show that new Stain-Ex outperforms the leading brand in laboratory tests. And it costs less per fluid ounce than Tidy!

Clearly, they've fixed their "costs less" claim. But what about their tests? Can you now safely believe that Stain-Ex is a better detergent than the leading brand?

Not necessarily. Again, what the ad says *sounds* great, but you have to remember that this *is* an ad, which means you have to question its credibility. Your questions should be all the more insistent because the ad doesn't tell you anything *about* the tests. You don't know, for example:

- Who conducted the studies?
- How were the studies conducted?
- What exactly was tested?
- What exactly were the results?

We'll spend a whole lesson talking about tests and studies later in the book. For now, however, it's important to remember that tests and studies can be manipulated to get specific results. In other words, it's important to have a healthy skepticism about tests, surveys, and studies. They should be accepted only as very tentative truths until you can find out the answers to the kind of questions asked above. I can say, for example, that "four out of five dentists surveyed recommend CleanRight toothpaste to their patients." In order for this claim to be true, all I have to do is survey five dentists—four of whom are my friends and who I know *do* recommend that toothpaste. Is my survey impartial? Certainly not. But I can now make this claim, and it sounds good to the consumer.

When analyzing studies, probably the most important thing to consider is who conducted the study. Why? Because knowing who conducts it can help determine whether or not it's legitimate. Do the conductors have anything at stake in the results? For example, if an independent consumer group conducted the Stain-Ex lab tests, would you feel better about accepting their claims as tentative truths? Absolutely; they're not very likely to be biased. But if the makers of Stain-Ex conducted the tests, the likelihood of bias is extremely high—you should be more skeptical about claims made by them.

In the real world, it's often a little more complicated than this, but you get the idea; studies and surveys are not always to be trusted.

Practice

Read the following claims carefully. Write **C** for complete and credible and **I** for incomplete or incredible.

_____ **4.** Recent taste tests prove Rich Chocolate Frosting tastes best.

_____ **5.** According to a Temple University study, three out of five Philadelphia shoppers surveyed have used their debit cards instead of cash to pay for groceries at their local supermarkets.

_____ **6.** A recent survey shows Americans prefer Choco-Bites to regular chocolate chip cookies.

Answers

4. I. First of all, the validity of the taste tests should be questioned. Secondly, "tastes best" is a vague phrase.

5. C. This claim is credible—it's complete and precise. Also, because it's a university study of supermarkets, there's little chance for bias. Furthermore, the claim acknowledges that it's only three out of five shoppers *surveyed*. That is, they're not trying to suggest that they surveyed everyone.

6. I. This claim is problematic. First is the vagueness of the statement "a recent survey." Second, what exactly are "regular" chocolate chip cookies?

▶ Averages

Recently, you heard someone on a talk show claim, "The average American teenager spends 29 hours per week watching television." What's wrong with this claim, other than the fact that it's a bit disturbing?

The trouble with this claim lies in the word *average*—a word often misused, and often used to mislead. Here, the problem for the listener becomes *defining* "average." What *is* the average American teenager? What age? What habits? What likes or dislikes? How we define "the average American teenager" can make a big difference in determining what this claim actually means.

Sometimes, using the word *average* to describe something is good enough—like the *average banana* for example. But often, average is in the eye of the beholder. My definition of an average teenager, for example, is probably quite different from my parents' definition, and both of our definitions are probably quite different from my 15-year-old cousin's idea of the average teen.

The word *average* can also be troublesome when we're talking about numbers. Take, for example, the following advertisement:

Looking for a safe, secure place to start a family? Then come to Serenity, Virginia. With an average of ten acres per lot, our properties provide your children with plenty of space to grow and play. Our spacious lawns, tree-lined streets, and friendly neighbors make Serenity a great place to grow up!

Sounds like a terrific place, doesn't it? Unfortunately, this ad is very misleading if you think you're going to move onto a big property.

In most cases, **average** means *mean*, the number reached by dividing the total number by the number of participants. Let's take a look at how Serenity came up with this number. Here are the facts:

In Serenity, there are 100 properties. Ten of those properties have 91 acres each. Ninety of those properties have only one acre each.

$$
\begin{array}{rl}
10 \times 91 = & 910 \\
90 \times 1 = & \underline{90} \\
& 1,000 \quad \text{(total acres)} \\
\div & \underline{100} \quad \text{(number of properties)} \\
& 10 \quad \text{(average acres per property)}
\end{array}
$$

Ten acres is the average, all right. But does that represent the majority? Does the average accurately suggest what most properties in Serenity are like? Obviously not. In Serenity, the typical house sits on just one acre, not ten.

It's important to keep in mind that *average* does not necessarily mean *typical* or *usual*. Unfortunately, that's generally what people think of when they hear the word *average*. And that's why an ad like this can be so misleading.

Practice

Read the following claims carefully to determine whether the use of the word *average* is acceptable or problematic. If the word is problematic, explain why.

7. The average woman lives a happier life than the average man.

8. The average life span of American women is two years longer than that of Canadian women.

9. The average salary at Wyntex Corporation is $75,000.

Answers

7. Very problematic. What is the "average" woman? The "average" man? Furthermore, how do you define "happier"? Happier in what way?

8. Acceptable.

9. Problematic. The salary range at a company like Wyntex can be so large that $75,000 may not represent the typical salary. If the president and CEO make $2 billion a year, for example, that clearly inflates the average. Meanwhile, most employees at the company may be making less than $40,000.

▶ In Short

Incomplete claims and half-truths can *look* and *sound* convincing. But a critical thinker like you has to be wary of such claims. When someone is trying to convince you to do something—as advertisers do hundreds of times each day, for instance—watch out for misleading claims that make their cases sound stronger than they really are.

Skill Building until Next Time

- Pick up a popular magazine and look for ads that make incomplete claims. Compare them to ads that show more respect for your judgment and give you more information.
- Listen carefully to others today at work, on the radio, or on TV. Do you hear any incomplete claims? Do you notice any suspicious "averages"?

6 ▶ What's in a Word?

LESSON SUMMARY

The words people use can have a powerful effect on their listeners. By choosing certain words instead of others or by phrasing questions in a way that is meant to elicit a specific response, people may try to influence your thoughts or actions. This lesson will show you how to recognize this kind of subtle persuasion.

our cousin likes to sky dive, mountain climb, and race cars. How would you describe him?

- Reckless
- Adventurous
- Free-spirited

As different as these words are, each one can be used to describe someone who engages in the above activities. The word you choose, however, depends upon your opinion of these activities. Clearly, *free-spirited* is the word with the most positive slant; *adventurous* is more or less neutral; and *reckless* is negative. Your word choice will convey a particular image of your cousin—whether you intend it to or not.

Words are powerful, and they can influence us without us even realizing it. That's because they carry at least two layers of meaning: denotation and connotation. **Denotation** is a word's exact or dictionary meaning. **Connotation** is the implied or suggested meaning, the emotional impact that the word carries. For example, *thin, slender,* and *lean* all mean essentially the same thing—their denotation is the same—but they have different connotations. *Slender* suggests a gracefulness that *thin* and *lean* do not. *Lean,* on the other hand, suggests a hardness or scarcity that *thin* and *slender* do not.

Denotation: the dictionary meaning of a word
Connotation: the emotional impact or implied meaning of a word

- Passed away
- Passed on
- Is no longer with us
- Expired
- Departed
- Deceased

Because words carry so much weight, advertisers, politicians, and anyone else who wants to convince you to believe one thing or another choose their words carefully. By using subtle persuasion techniques, they can often manipulate feelings and influence reactions so that viewers and listeners don't realize they're being swayed. The best way to prevent this kind of influence is to be aware of these techniques. If you can recognize them, they lose their power. It's like watching a magician on stage once you already know the secret behind his tricks. You appreciate his art, but you're no longer under his spell.

There are three different subtle persuasion techniques we'll discuss in this lesson: *euphemisms, dysphemisms,* and *biased questions.*

▶ Euphemisms and Dysphemisms

Euphemisms are the most common of the subtle persuasion techniques. You've probably even used them yourself many times without even realizing it. A euphemism is when a phrase—usually one that's harsh, negative, or offensive—is replaced with a milder or more positive expression.

For example, there are many ways to say that someone has died. *Die* itself is a neutral word—it expresses the fact of death straightforwardly without any real *mood* attached to it. However, this word is often softened by replacing it with a euphemism, such as one of the following:

Just as we can say *died* in a softer or more positive way—a way that suggests movement to a better place, for example—we can also say it in a cruder or more negative way, like one of the following:

- Croaked
- Kicked the bucket
- Bit the dust

When we replace a positive or neutral expression with one that is negative or unpleasant, we're using a **dysphemism.**

Euphemism: a milder or more positive expression used to replace a negative or unpleasant one
Dysphemism: replacing a neutral or positive expression with a negative or unpleasant one

Euphemisms and dysphemisms are used more than ever these days, especially in advertising, the media, and by politicians to influence our thoughts and feelings. Take, for example, the phrase *used cars.* Used car dealers used to sell *used cars*—now they sell *previously owned vehicles.* See the euphemism? The more pleasant phrase *previously owned* doesn't carry the suggestion of someone else *using*—just *owning.*

Euphemisms are used a great deal in political and social issues. If you oppose abortion, for example, then you are *pro-life.* If you support the right to abort, on the other hand, you're *pro-choice.* See how important these euphemisms are? How could someone be *against* life? *Against* choice?

Practice

Read each of the words or phrases below and write a euphemism and dysphemism for each.

1. medical practitioner

2. odor

3. geriatric

Answers

There are many possible answers. Here are a few:

	Euphemism	Dysphemism
1.	healer	butcher
2.	fragrance	stench
3.	elderly	ancient

Practice

Read sentences 4–7 carefully. If you notice a euphemism, write an **E** in the blank. If you notice a dysphemism, write a **D**. If the sentence is neutral, write **N**.

_____ **4.** Al saved a lot of money on his taxes this year with his creative accounting techniques.

_____ **5.** She is very good at taking care of details.

_____ **6.** He's not crazy; he's just a little unusual, that's all.

_____ **7.** I'm off to see my shrink.

Answers

4. E "creative accounting techniques"
5. N
6. E "a little unusual"
7. D "shrink"

▶ Biased Questions

Imagine someone stops you on the street and asks you to participate in a survey about tax cuts. You agree, and she asks you the following questions:

- Do you support tax cuts that benefit only the wealthy and neglect the needs of those with low incomes?
- Do you think the government should be allowed to make tax cuts that exclude the poor and uneducated?

No matter how you feel about tax cuts, chances are you can't answer anything but *no* to these questions. Why? Because if you say *yes*, it sounds like you are not empathetic to the needs of those who are helpless. These questions are phrased unfairly, making it difficult for you to give a fair answer. In other words, inherent in the questions is a certain attitude toward tax cuts—in this case, a negative one—that *prejudices* the questions. In short, the questions aren't fair—they're biased.

Notice how these particular questions use dysphemisms to bias the questions and pressure you to answer them a certain way. In this example, *tax cuts* become equivalent to negative terms such as *neglect* and *exclude*.

EXAMPLES OF EUPHEMISMS AND DYSPHEMISMS		
WORD OR PHRASE	**EUPHEMISM**	**DYSPHEMISM**
fan	aficionado	zealot
inexpensive	economical	cheap
grandstander	public servant	lackey
old maid	bachelorette	spinster

Here is how euphemisms might be used to bias the questions toward the opposing point of view:

- Do you support tax cuts that will benefit all socioeconomic levels of society and help improve the economy?
- Do you think the government should be allowed to make tax cuts that give people's hard-earned money back to them?

This time, notice how saying *yes* is much easier than saying *no*. If you say *no* to the first question, it sounds like you are indifferent to what happens to you and your society. If you say *no* to the second question, it sounds like you are without compassion and don't believe that people deserve to keep what they earn.

Here are the questions revised once again so that you can answer *yes* or *no* fairly:

- Do you support tax cuts?
- Do you think the government should be allowed to decide when to make tax cuts?

Professional surveys will be careful to ask fair questions, but when political organizations, advertisers, and other groups or individuals have an agenda, they may use biased questions to elicit specific results. Similarly, anyone who wants to influence you may use biased questions to get you to respond in a certain way. That's why it's important for you to recognize when a question is fair and when it's biased.

Practice

Read the following questions carefully. If you think the question is biased, write a **B** in the blank. If you think it's unbiased, write a **U**.

_____ **8.** What did you think of that lousy movie?

_____ **9.** Do you think the driving age should be raised to eighteen?

_____ **10.** Are you going to vote to reelect that crooked politician for governor?

_____ **11.** Do you support the destruction of rain forests rich in natural resources so that wealthy companies can flourish?

_____ **12.** Should medical marijuana be legalized?

Answers

8. B. The word *lousy* makes it hard to say you liked it; you'd be admitting to liking lousy films.

9. U

10. B. Most people probably would not feel comfortable answering *yes* to this question.

11. B. A *yes* answer means you support the destruction of natural resources.

12. U

Practice

To further improve your critical thinking and reasoning skills, take each of the unbiased questions from items 8–12 and turn them into biased questions. Then do the opposite: Take the biased questions and turn them into fair questions. Write your answers on a separate piece of paper.

Answers

Your answers will vary, but your revised questions should look something like this:

8. What did you think of that movie?

9. Don't you think that teenagers are too irresponsible to be allowed to drive until they're eighteen?

10. Are you going to vote to reelect the governor?

11. Do you support rainforest harvesting?

12. Do you think that medical marijuana, which dramatically relieves the pain and suffering of cancer and glaucoma patients, should be legalized?

▶ In Short

Euphemisms, dysphemisms, and *biased questions* can have a powerful influence on readers and listeners. Euphemisms replace negative expressions with ones that are neutral or positive. Dysphemisms do the opposite: They replace neutral or positive expressions with ones that are harsh or negative. Biased questions make it difficult for us to answer questions fairly. Learning to recognize these subtle persuasion techniques promotes independent thinking and lets people come to their own conclusions, rather than the conclusions others want them to reach.

Skill Building until Next Time

- Listen carefully to conversations, to the news, to what people say to you and ask of you. Do you notice any euphemisms, dysphemisms, or biased questions? Do you catch yourself using any of these techniques yourself?
- You can improve your ability to recognize subtle persuasion techniques by practicing them yourself. Come up with euphemisms, dysphemisms, and biased questions throughout the day.

7 ▶ Working with Arguments

LESSON SUMMARY

You hear arguments of all kinds throughout the day. In this lesson, you'll learn how to recognize the components of a deductive argument and how it differs from an inductive argument.

Consider the following conversation:
"Junior, time to go to bed."
"But why?"
"Because I said so!"

Only a parent can get away with giving the answer "because I said so." But even parents sometimes have trouble using this approach to make a convincing argument. It's important to provide qualifiable reasons for asking someone to accept a claim or take a certain action. Providing qualifiable reasons is the best way to *support* your argument.

In the next three lessons, you're going to learn about **deductive arguments**: what they are, how they work, and how to recognize (and make) a good deductive argument—one that supports its assertions.

First, you need to know what *deductive reasoning* is. To help define it, the counterpart of deductive reasoning, which is *inductive reasoning,* will be introduced first.

► Inductive Reasoning

When detectives arrive at the scene of a crime, the first thing they do is look for clues that can help them piece together what happened. A broken window, for example, might suggest how a burglar entered or exited. Likewise, the fact that an intruder didn't disturb anything but a painting that hid a safe might suggest that the burglar knew exactly where the safe was hidden. And this, in turn, suggests that the burglar knew the victim.

The process described above is called **inductive reasoning.** It consists of making observations and then drawing conclusions based on those observations.

Like a detective, you use inductive reasoning all the time in your daily life. You might notice, for example, that every time you eat a hot dog with chili and onions, you get a stomachache. Using inductive reasoning, you could logically conclude that the chili dogs cause indigestion, and that you should probably stop eating them. Similarly, you might notice that your cat tries to scratch you every time you rub her stomach. You could logically conclude that she does not like her stomach rubbed. In both examples, what you're doing is moving from the *specific*—a particular observation—to the *general*—a larger conclusion. Inductive reasoning starts from observation and evidence and leads to a conclusion.

Using inductive reasoning generally involves the following questions:

1. What have you observed? What evidence is available?
2. What can you conclude from that evidence?
3. Is that *conclusion* logical?

We'll come back to these questions in a later lesson. For now, you know enough about inductive reasoning to see how deductive reasoning differs from it.

► Deductive Reasoning

Unlike inductive reasoning, which moves from *specific evidence* to a *general conclusion*, **deductive reasoning** does the opposite; it generally moves from a *conclusion* to the *evidence* for that conclusion. In inductive reasoning, the conclusion has to be "figured out" and we must determine whether or not the conclusion is valid. In deductive reasoning, on the other hand, we start with the conclusion and then see if the *evidence* for that conclusion is valid. Generally, if the evidence is valid, the conclusion it supports is valid as well. In other words, deductive reasoning involves asking:

1. What is the conclusion?
2. What evidence supports it?
3. Is that *evidence* logical?

If you can answer yes to question 3, then the conclusion should be logical and the argument sound.

It's easy to confuse inductive and deductive reasoning, so here's something to help you remember which is which:

Inductive: **E**vidence • **C**onclusion (IEC)
Deductive: **C**onclusion • **E**vidence (DCE)

Inductive reasoning starts with the evidence and moves to the conclusion. Deductive reasoning begins with the conclusion and moves to the evidence for that conclusion. Here's a memory trick to help you: You can remember that the word *Inductive* begins with a vowel, as does *Evidence,* so in inductive reasoning, you start with the evidence. *Deductive* begins with a consonant, and so does *Conclusion,* which is where you begin in deductive reasoning.

In the field of logic, deductive reasoning includes *formal* (mathematical or symbolic) logic such as syllogisms and truth tables. Some practice with formal logic will certainly sharpen your critical thinking and reasoning skills, but this book won't cover that kind of logic. Instead, we will continue to focus on *informal* logic—that is, the kind of critical thinking and reasoning skills that help you solve problems, assess and defend arguments, and make effective decisions in your daily life.

The Parts of a Deductive Argument

Lesson 2, "Problem-Solving Strategies," talked about the importance of identifying the main issue in order to solve a problem. You learned to ask yourself, "What is the real problem to be solved here?" Then you took that problem and broke it down into its parts.

In looking at deductive arguments, you should follow a similar process. First, you should identify the conclusion. The **conclusion** is the main claim or point the argument is trying to make. The various pieces of evidence that support that conclusion are called **premises**. Keep in mind that an argument is not necessarily a fight. In talking about inductive and deductive reasoning, an **argument** refers to a claim that is supported by evidence. Whether or not that evidence is good is another matter!

Identifying the conclusion is often more difficult than you might expect, because conclusions can sometimes seem like premises, and vice versa. Another difficulty is that you're used to thinking of conclusions as coming at the end of something. But in deductive arguments, the conclusion can appear anywhere. Thus, when someone presents you with a deductive argument, the first thing you should do is ask yourself:

"What is the main claim, or overall idea, that the argument is trying to prove?"

In other words, just as a problem is often composed of many parts, the conclusion in a deductive argument is often composed of many premises. So it's important to keep in mind the "big picture."

Claim:	assertion about the truth, existence, or value of something
Argument:	a claim supported by evidence
Conclusion:	the main claim or point in an argument
Premises:	pieces of evidence that support the conclusion

The Structure of Deductive Arguments

The conclusion in a deductive argument can be supported by premises in two different ways. Say you have an argument with three premises supporting the conclusion. In one type of deductive argument, each premise provides its own individual support for the conclusion. That is, each premise alone is evidence for that main claim. In the other type of argument, the premises work together to support the conclusion. That is, they work like a chain of ideas to support the argument. These two types of arguments are represented as diagrams below.

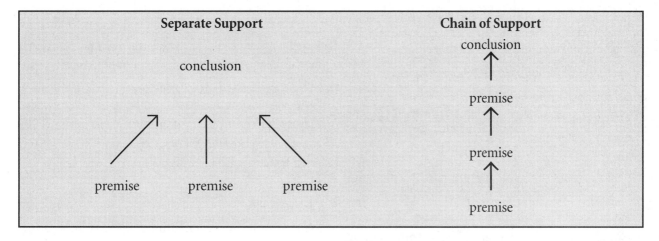

Separate Support	**Chain of Support**
conclusion	conclusion
premise premise premise	premise
	premise
	premise

Here's how these two structures might look in a real argument:

Separate support: You shouldn't take that job. The pay is lousy, the hours are terrible, and there are no benefits.

You shouldn't take that job.

| Lousy pay | Terrible hours | No benefits |

Chain support: You shouldn't take that job. The pay is lousy, which will make it hard for you to pay your bills, and that will make you unhappy.

You shouldn't take that job.

↑

and that will make you unhappy

↑

which will make it hard for you to pay your bills

↑

the pay is lousy

Notice how in the second version, the entire argument builds upon one idea, the lousy pay, whereas in the first, the argument is built upon three separate ideas. Both, however, are equally logical.

Of course, an argument can have both separate and chain support. We'll see an example of that shortly. What's important now is to understand that when premises depend upon each other, as they do in the chain support structure, what we really have is a chain of premises and conclusions. Look how the layers of a chain support argument work:

Conclusion:	It will be hard to pay your bills.
Premise:	The pay is lousy.
Conclusion:	That will make you unhappy.

Premise:	It will be hard to pay your bills.
Premise:	That will make you unhappy.
Overall conclusion:	You shouldn't take that job.

Because deductive arguments often work this way, it's very important to be able to distinguish the *overall* conclusion from the conclusions that may be used in the chain of support.

► Identifying the Overall Conclusion

Read the following sentences:

He's tall, so he must be a good basketball player. All tall people are good basketball players.

These two sentences represent a small deductive argument. It's not a particularly *good* argument, but it is a good example of deductive structure. If these two sentences are broken down into their parts, three different claims arise:

1. He's tall.
2. He must be a good basketball player.
3. All tall people are good basketball players.

Now ask the key question: "What is this argument trying to prove?" In other words, what is the conclusion?

Two clues should help you come up with the right answer. First, look at which claims have support (evidence) in this example. Is there anything here to support the claim that "He is tall"? No. Is there anything to support the claim, "All tall people are good basketball players"? No. But there *are* premises to support the claim, "He must be a good basketball player." Why must he be a good basketball player? Because:

1. He is tall.
2. All tall people are good basketball players.

Therefore, the conclusion of this argument is: "He must be a good basketball player." That is what the writer is trying to prove. The premises that support this conclusion are "He is tall" and "All tall people are good basketball players."

A second clue in the conclusion that "He must be a good basketball player" is the word *so*. Several key words and phrases indicate that a conclusion will follow. Similarly, certain words and phrases indicate that a premise will follow:

Indicate a Conclusion:	Indicate a Premise:
■ Accordingly	■ As indicated by
■ As a result	■ As shown by
■ Consequently	■ Because
■ Hence	■ For
■ It follows that	■ Given that
■ So	■ Inasmuch as
■ That's why	■ Since
■ Therefore	■ The reason is that
■ This shows/means/ suggests that	
■ Thus	

Now, are the premises that support the conclusion, "He must be a good basketball player," separate support or chain support?

You should be able to see that these premises *work together* to support the conclusion. "He is tall" alone doesn't support the conclusion, and neither does "All tall people are good basketball players." But the two premises together provide support for the conclusion. Thus, the example is considered a *chain of support* argument.

The Position of the Conclusion

While you might be used to thinking of the conclusion as something that comes at the end, in a deductive argument, the conclusion can appear in different places. Here is the same argument rearranged in several different ways:

- He must be a good basketball player. After all, he's tall, and all tall people are good basketball players.
- All tall people are good basketball players. Since he's tall, he must be a good basketball player.
- He's tall, and all tall people are good basketball players. He must be a good basketball player.
- He must be a good basketball player. After all, all tall people are good basketball players, and he's tall.
- All tall people are good basketball players. He must be a good basketball player because he's tall.

In larger deductive arguments, especially the kind found in articles and essays, the conclusion will often be stated before any premises. But it's important to remember that the conclusion can appear anywhere in the argument. The key is to keep in mind what the argument *as a whole* is trying to prove.

One way to test that you've found the right conclusion is to use the "because" test. If you've chosen the right claim, you should be able to put *because* between it and all of the other premises. Thus:

He must be a good basketball player **because** he's tall and **because** all tall people are good basketball players.

Practice

Read the following short arguments carefully. First, separate the arguments into claims by putting a slash mark (/) between each claim. Then, identify the claim that represents the *conclusion* in each deductive argument by underlining that claim.

Example: We should go to the park. It's a beautiful day, and besides, I need some exercise.

We should go to the park. / It's a beautiful day / and besides, I need some exercise.

1. The roads are icy and it's starting to snow heavily. Stay in the guest bedroom tonight. You can leave early in the morning.

2. She's smart and she has integrity. She'd make a great councilwoman. You should vote for her.

3. I don't think you should drive. You'd better give me your keys. You had a lot to drink tonight.

4. You really should stop smoking. Smoking causes lung cancer and emphysema. It makes your clothes and breath smell like smoke. Besides, it's a waste of money.

Answers

Before you check your answers, use the "because" test to see if you've correctly identified the conclusion.

1. The roads are icy / and it's starting to snow heavily. / <u>Stay in the guest bedroom tonight</u>. / You can leave early in the morning.

2. She's smart / and she has integrity. / She'd make a great councilwoman. / <u>You should vote for her</u>.

3. I don't think you should drive. / <u>You'd better give me your keys.</u> / You had a lot to drink tonight.

4. <u>You really should stop smoking.</u> / Smoking causes lung cancer and emphysema. / It makes your clothes and breath smell like smoke. / Besides, it's a waste of money.

Practice

For each argument in items 1–4, identify whether the premises work as separate support or chain support.

Answers

1. Separate. Three separate premises support the conclusion.

2. Separate and chain. "She's smart" and "she has integrity" are two separate claims that support the premise, "She'd make a great councilwoman." That premise, in turn, supports the conclusion.

3. Chain. The last premise, "You had a lot to drink tonight," supports the first, which in turn supports the conclusion.

4. Separate. Three separate premises support the conclusion.

▶ In Short

Unlike inductive arguments, which move from evidence to conclusion, deductive arguments move from the conclusion to evidence for that conclusion. The **conclusion** is the overall claim or main point of the argument, and the claims that support the conclusion are called **premises.** Deductive arguments can be supported by premises that work alone (separate support) or together (chain of support).

Skill Building until Next Time

- When you hear an argument, ask yourself whether it is an inductive or deductive argument. Did the person move from evidence to conclusion, or conclusion to evidence? If the argument is too complex to analyze this way, try choosing just one part of the argument and see whether it's inductive or deductive.
- When you come across deductive arguments today, try to separate the conclusion from the premises. Then consider whether the premises offer separate or chain support.

8 ▶ Evaluating Evidence

LESSON SUMMARY

Since it's the *evidence* in a deductive argument that makes the conclusion valid, it's important to evaluate that evidence. This lesson will show you how to check premises for two key factors: credibility and reasonableness.

ow that you're able to separate the conclusion from the premises that support it, it's time to *evaluate* those premises. This is a vital step; the conclusion, after all, is trying to convince you of something—that you should accept a certain opinion, change your beliefs, or take a specific action. Before you accept that conclusion, therefore, you need to examine the *validity* of the evidence for that conclusion.

Specifically, there are three questions to ask yourself when evaluating evidence:

1. What type of evidence is offered?
2. Is that evidence *credible*?
3. Is that evidence *reasonable*?

▶ Types of Evidence

There are many different types of evidence that can be offered in support of a conclusion. One of the most basic distinctions to make is between premises that are fact, premises that are opinion, and premises that can be accepted only as tentative truths.

Before going any further, here's a review of the difference between fact and opinion:

- A **fact** is something known for certain to have happened, to be true, or to exist.
- An **opinion** is something believed to have happened, to be true, or to exist.
- A **tentative truth** is a claim that may be a fact but that needs to be verified.

Whether they're facts, opinions, or tentative truths, premises can come in the following forms:

- Statistics or figures
- Physical evidence (artifacts)
- Things seen, felt, or heard (observations)
- Statements from experts and expert witnesses
- Reports of experiences
- Ideas, feelings, or beliefs

Of course, some types of evidence seem more convincing than others. That is, people are often more likely to believe or be convinced by statistics than by someone's opinion. But that doesn't mean that all statistics should automatically be accepted and that all opinions should be rejected. Because statistics can be manipulated and because opinions can be quite reasonable, all forms of evidence need to be examined for both credibility and reasonableness.

For example, the *reasonableness* of statistics can't really be questioned, but their *credibility* must be questioned. Similarly, any feeling or belief should be examined for both credibility *and* reasonableness.

▶ Is the Evidence Credible?

Whatever the type of evidence the arguer offers, the first thing that needs to be considered is the credibility of the arguer. Is the person making the argument credible? Second, if the arguer offers evidence from other sources, the credibility of those sources needs to be questioned. If both the arguer and his or her sources are credible, then the argument can tentatively be accepted. If not, the argument shouldn't be accepted until it is examined further.

First, here's a review of the criteria that determine credibility. To be credible, a source must:

- Be free of bias
- Have expertise

Expertise is determined by:

- Education
- Experience
- Job or position
- Reputation
- Achievements

In the case of an eyewitness account, the following must be considered:

- The witness's potential for bias
- The environment
- The physical and mental condition of the witness
- The time between the event and recollection of the event

Here is a short deductive argument. Read the following passage carefully:

Current statistics show that 15% of children are obese. Childhood obesity increases the risk for developing high blood pressure, Type 2 diabetes, and coronary heart disease. In fact, 80% of children diagnosed with Type 2 diabetes are overweight. Being obese also lowers children's self-esteem and affects their relationships with their peers. This growing epidemic can be attributed to several factors: genetics, lack of physical activity—children are spending more and more time in front of the television and the computer—and lack of nutritional education. If children were educated about nutrition and exercise, then obesity rates would decline significantly. That's why we must pass a law that requires that nutrition and exercise education be part of the school curriculum for all students in grades K–12. Unfortunately, it's too late for my 12-year-old brother; he's already been diagnosed with Type 2 diabetes. But we must take measures to improve the health and well-being of future generations to come.

*This and other statistics in the rest of the text are fictitious and meant to serve purely as examples.

First, identify the conclusion in this passage. What is the overall claim or point that the passage is trying to prove? Once you identify the conclusion, underline it.

You should have underlined the claim, "We must pass a law that requires that nutrition and exercise education be part of the school curriculum for all students in grades K–12." The phrase "That's why" may have helped you identify this idea as the main claim. (If you had trouble, take a moment to review Lesson 7, "Working with Arguments.") The following table lists the premises that support this conclusion. Note that not every sentence in this argument is a premise.

The arguer's experience offers an important clue here about *her* credibility. Because of what happened to her brother, is she likely to be biased on the issue? Absolutely. However, does this rule her out as a credible arguer? Not necessarily. Chances are that if her brother was diagnosed with diabetes due to poor nutritional habits, she knows more about the issue than the average person. In other words, her experience indicates that she has some level of expertise in the area. Thus, though there's evidence of some bias, there's also evidence of some expertise. Because there is both bias and expertise, the argument needs to be examined further before you can determine whether or not to accept it.

Is the arguer's experience credible? Well, it can be assumed that she's telling the truth about her brother being diagnosed. Is her opinion credible? That depends on her own credibility, which is still in question, and the reasonableness of that opinion, which is covered in the next section.

The next step is to consider the credibility of premises provided by the outside source; that is, the statistics offered about childhood obesity. Notice that here the arguer doesn't give a source for the figures that she provides. This should automatically raise a red flag. Because numbers can so easily be manipulated and misleading, it's crucial to know the source of any figures offered in support of an argument.

PREMISES THAT SUPPORT THE CONCLUSION	
TYPE OF PREMISE	PREMISE
Opinion	If children were educated about nutrition and exercise, then obesity rates would decline significantly.
Statistics	Current statistics show that 15% of children are obese. In fact, 80% of children diagnosed with Type 2 diabetes are overweight.
Experience	Unfortunately, it's too late for my 12-year-old brother; he's already been diagnosed with Type 2 diabetes.

Practice

1. Which of the following sources for the statistic would you find most credible, and why?
   a. Parents against Obesity
   b. National Institute of Health Statistics
   c. The makers of SweetSnackPacks for Kids

Answer

The most credible source is **b**, the National Institute of Health Statistics. Of these three sources, the National Institute of Health Statistics is by far the least biased. Parents against Obesity has a position on children's nutritional education initiatives (for them), as do the makers of SweetSnackPacks for Kids (most likely against them).

▶ Is the Evidence Reasonable?

Now that you've considered the credibility of the arguer and the evidence she's offered, the next question you should ask is whether or not the evidence is *reasonable*. This question relates mostly to evidence in the form of opinions and tentative truths.

Remember that **reasonable** means *logical*: according to conclusions drawn from evidence or common sense. So whenever evidence comes in the form of an opinion or tentative truth, you need to consider how reasonable that premise is. Read this opinion:

If children were educated about nutrition and exercise, then obesity rates would decline significantly.

Does this seem like a reasonable opinion to you? Why or why not?

However you feel about nutritional education programs, there *is* some sense to this opinion. After all, if children were educated about nutrition and exercise, it seems logical that they would eat healthier and exercise more, thereby reducing obesity rates. Common sense, right?

But this opinion isn't a conclusion drawn from *evidence*. Look how much stronger this premise would be if it added *evidence* to *common sense*:

If children were educated about nutrition and exercise, then obesity rates would decline significantly. For example, in Toledo, Ohio, all schools in 1999 implemented nutrition and exercise education programs into the curriculum for grades K–12. As a result, obesity rates in children ages 6–11 dropped from 15% in 1999 to 10% in 2004.

Notice that this statistic is used to support the opinion, which is then used to support the conclusion. In other words, this premise is part of a chain of support.

Opinions, then, can be reasonable either because they're based on common sense or because they're drawn from evidence, like what happened in Toledo. Of course, if an opinion is reasonable on *both* accounts, it's that much stronger as support for the conclusion.

Practice

Read the following opinions carefully. Are they reasonable? If so, is the reasonableness based on logic, common sense, or evidence?

2. You should quit smoking. The smoke in your lungs can't be good for you.

3. You should quit smoking. The Surgeon General says that it causes lung cancer, emphysema, and shortness of breath.

4. Don't listen to him. He's a jerk.

5. Don't listen to him. He gave me the same advice and it almost got me fired.

Answers

2. Reasonable, based on common sense.

3. Reasonable, based on evidence; in this case, on an expert's opinion.

4. Unreasonable. Because this is a deductive argument where the premise is unreasonable, the whole argument should be rejected as unreasonable.

5. Reasonable, based on evidence; in this case, on experience.

Practice

6. Reread the argument from the last lesson:

He's tall, so he must be a good basketball player. All tall people are good basketball players.

Are the premises in this argument reasonable? Why or why not?

Answer

No, the premises in this argument are not reasonable, and therefore, the conclusion is not reasonable, either. Why not? Because common sense should tell you that you can't make big generalizations like "All tall people are good basketball players." You should beware of any premise that makes a claim about *all* or *none*. There is almost always an exception.

▶ In Short

Premises can come in many forms, from statistics to feelings or opinions. When evaluating evidence, it's necessary to examine credibility and reasonableness: the credibility of the arguer, the credibility of any sources, and the reasonableness of each premise.

Skill Building until Next Time

- As you hear deductive arguments throughout the day, pay attention to what type of evidence is offered in support of the conclusion. Statistics? Experiences? Opinions?
- Consider the credibility of the people who present you with deductive arguments today. Could they be biased? What is their level of expertise? If they offer other sources to support their arguments, are those sources credible?

Recognizing a Good Argument

LESSON SUMMARY

There are many components of a *good* argument—one that is convincing for good reason. This lesson will show you how to recognize and make a strong deductive argument.

Y
ou got laid off from your job two months ago. You've been looking for another job but haven't had much luck. But the company you interviewed with yesterday just made you an offer. The pay isn't that good, but you're thinking about taking the job anyway; you need the money. Your friend, however, tells you not to take it: "The pay is lousy, the hours are terrible, and there are no benefits," he says. "Don't do it." Should you listen to your friend? Has he made a good argument? How can you tell?

You already know what a deductive argument is. You know how to separate the conclusion from the evidence. And you know how to evaluate the evidence. These are essential steps in analyzing a deductive argument. But in order to determine the overall strength of an argument, there are several other criteria to take into consideration. Specifically, in a good deductive argument:

- The conclusion and premises are clear and complete.
- The conclusion and premises are free of excessive subtle persuasion.
- The premises are credible and reasonable.
- The premises are sufficient and substantive.
- The argument considers the other side.

You should already be familiar with the first three criteria, so we'll just take a moment to review them before we address the last two.

▶ Clear and Complete

In Lesson 5, "Partial Claims and Half-Truths," you learned how to recognize hidden agendas. In order for a deductive argument to carry weight, its conclusion must be clear and complete; there should be no doubt about the claim being made. The same goes for the premises; if a comparison isn't fair or if what is being compared isn't clear, that claim cannot be valid. Evidence can't be reasonable if it is incomplete.

▶ Free of Excessive Subtle Persuasion

In Lesson 6, "What's in a Word?" you learned about euphemisms, dysphemisms, and biased questions. These subtle persuasion techniques are indeed manipulative, but they're not the ultimate sin when it comes to arguments. It's natural for people to choose words that will have a certain impact on their listeners. It's natural, for example, for the government to use the phrase "military campaign" if they don't want to raise protests about going to war. In other words, the *occasional* euphemism, dysphemism, or *mildly* biased question can be forgiven. But if an argument is loaded with these persuasive techniques, you should analyze it carefully. Generally, arguments that are laden with euphemisms, dysphemisms, and biased questions are this way because they lack reasonable and credible evidence. In other words, the arguer may be trying to persuade you with language rather than reason because he or she lacks evidence. Excessive use of subtle persuasion can also indicate that the arguer is biased about the issue.

▶ Credible and Reasonable Premises

As discussed in the previous lesson, the two criteria for good evidence are *credibility* and *reasonableness*. Evidence is credible when it is free of bias and when the sources have a respectable level of expertise. Evidence is reasonable when it is logical, drawn from evidence or common sense.

▶ Sufficient and Substantive Premises

You ask a coworker about the restaurant that recently opened down the street. He tells you, "The Hot Tamale Café? Don't eat there. The service is lousy."

Has he given you a good argument? Well, the conclusion, "Don't eat there," is clear and complete. The premise that supports the conclusion, "The service is lousy," is also clear and complete. The premise and conclusion are free from subtle persuasion. The premise is reasonable, and we don't have any reason to doubt credibility—he's given good recommendations about places to eat before. But is this a good argument? Not really.

Though all of the other criteria check out, this argument has a very important weakness: It simply doesn't offer enough evidence. Not enough reasons are given to accept the conclusion. So, the service is lousy. But maybe the food, the ambiance, and the prices are excellent. When there are so many other reasons for going to a restaurant, just one premise to support that conclusion is not enough.

Here's a much better argument. What makes it better is the number of premises offered to support the conclusion. Some premises are separate support, and some are offered to support other premises (chains of support).

Don't eat at that restaurant. The service is lousy. They messed up our orders and we had to wait 15 minutes even though there were empty tables. The food is overpriced, too. A plain hamburger is $12.50! The place is dirty—we had to wipe our table down twice with napkins, and I saw a dead cockroach in the corner. And there is no décor to speak of—just bright blue walls and a poster of Hawaii in the corner, even though it's a Mexican restaurant.

Now *this* restaurant sounds like a place to avoid, doesn't it? What's good about this argument is not only that it offers several distinct premises that separately support the conclusion (**major premises**), but it also offers support (**minor premises**) for each of those premises. Each major premise is followed by a specific detail that supports *that* premise. Here's how this argument maps out:

Conclusion:	Don't eat at that restaurant.
Major premise:	The service is lousy.
Minor premise:	They messed up our orders.
Minor premise:	We had to wait 15 minutes even though there were empty tables.
Major premise:	The food is overpriced.
Minor premise:	A plain hamburger is $12.50!
Major premise:	The place is dirty.
Minor premise:	We had to wipe our table down twice with napkins.
Minor premise:	I saw a dead cockroach in the corner.
Major premise:	There is no décor.
Minor premise:	just bright blue walls and a poster of Hawaii in the corner, even though it's a Mexican restaurant.

Practice

1. Take the following argument and make it substantial. Provide more evidence by adding major and minor supporting premises:

Public school students should wear uniforms just like private school students do. Uniforms will create a stronger sense of community.

Stronger argument:

Answer

Your answer will vary depending upon what premises you chose to support this argument. At any rate, your argument should be significantly longer than the first version. Here's one revision that provides several major and minor premises to support the conclusion. The major premises are in bold.

Public school students should wear uniforms just like private school students do. For one thing, **uniforms will create a stronger sense of community**. It's important for children to feel like they belong, and uniforms are a powerful physical and psychological way to create that sense of belonging. **Uniforms also improve discipline**. According to the Department of Education, private schools across the country have fewer discipline problems than public schools, and the handful of public schools that have experimented with uniforms have found that their discipline problems decreased sharply. Furthermore, **uniforms can help increase the self-esteem of children from low-income families.** If everyone wears the same clothes, they don't have to come to school ashamed of their hand-me-downs or second-hand clothing.

▶ Considering the Other Side

At the beginning of this lesson, your friend tried to talk you out of taking that job offer. Did he provide a good argument based on the criteria we've discussed so far? Here's his argument again to refresh your memory:

"The pay is lousy, the hours are terrible, and there are no benefits," he says. "Don't do it."

Well, his argument is reasonable, credible, free of subtle persuasion, and he offers three different reasons, though they could be supported with specific details (minor premises). Still, this argument lacks one criterion of a good argument; it does not consider counterarguments.

Counterarguments are those arguments that might be offered by someone arguing for the other side. That is, if you are arguing that it's better to live in the city than in the country, you need to keep in mind what someone arguing that living in the country is better than living in the city might think. By considering counterarguments, you show your critical thinking skills—whatever your opinion, you have considered all sides of the issue. And this helps demonstrate your credibility, too; it shows that you've done your homework, that you obviously know something about the issue.

For example, when you hear your friend's argument, what thoughts might go through your mind? You might come up with the following reasons to *take* the job rather than reject it:

- You really need the money.
- You can advance quickly.
- You'll have benefits after six months.
- You can switch to a different shift after six months.
- It's a lot closer to home than your previous job.

If your friend really wants to convince you not to take the job, he'll not only support his conclusion with credible, reasonable, and ample evidence, he'll also show that he knows why you might want to say yes—and why his reasons for saying no are better.

One way to help you develop a better argument is to play devil's advocate. When you're getting ready to make an argument, write down your conclusion and your premises, and then do the same for the *opposite* position. You might want to pretend you are in court and you are both the prosecution and the defense. This will help you anticipate what the other side will say and therefore you can come up with a premise to *counter* that argument. Here's how your friend might revise his argument if he considered the other side:

Don't take that job. I know you really need the money, but the pay is lousy. It's a full three dollars less per hour than your last job. You can probably move through the ranks quickly, but because you'd be starting at a lower pay scale, you'd have to take several steps just to get back up to your old salary. And you have to wait six months before you can switch shifts and get benefits. What if something happens in the meantime? True, you'll save time and gas because it's closer, but is that extra thirty minutes a day worth it?

Notice two things that your friend does here. First, he systematically and carefully acknowledges each of your concerns. Second, he counters each of those concerns with a reasonable premise. Furthermore, he improved his argument by adding specific minor premises, like the fact that the pay is three dollars less per hour.

Now it's your turn.

Practice

The school uniform argument is reprinted below. Play devil's advocate and make a list of counterarguments. Then rewrite the argument to make it stronger.

Public school students should wear uniforms just like private school students do. For one thing, **uniforms will create a stronger sense of community**. It's important for children to feel like they belong, and uniforms are a powerful physical and psychological way to create that sense of belonging. **Uniforms also improve discipline.** According to the Department of Education, private schools across the country have fewer discipline problems than public schools, and the handful of public schools that have experimented with uniforms have found that their discipline problems decreased sharply. Furthermore, **uniforms can help increase the self-esteem of children from low-income families.** If everyone wears the same clothes, they don't have to come to school ashamed of their hand-me-downs or second-hand clothing.

2. Counterarguments:

3. Revised argument:

Answers

Your counterarguments might look something like the following:

   a. Uniforms won't create a stronger sense of community; they'll create a culture of conformity.

   b. Uniforms alone won't decrease discipline problems. The problem goes deeper than that.

   c. Students from low-income families will still have less expensive shoes, coats, etc. Uniforms alone can't hide their socioeconomic status.

Your revised argument depends upon your counterarguments. Here's how the counterarguments might be incorporated. The sentences that address counterarguments are in bold.

Public school students should wear uniforms just like private school students do. For one thing, uniforms will create a stronger sense of community. It's important for children to feel like they belong, and uniforms are a powerful physical and psychological way to create that sense of belonging. **While some worry that uniforms encourage conformity, a sense of belonging helps give students the self-esteem they need to find their individuality.** Uniforms also improve discipline. According to the Department of Education, private schools across the country have fewer discipline problems than public schools, and the handful of public schools that have experimented with uniforms have found that their discipline problems decreased sharply. **This demonstrates that uniforms alone can have a profound affect on discipline.** Furthermore, uniforms can help increase the self-esteem of children from low-income families. If everyone wears the same clothes, they don't have to come to school ashamed of their hand-me-downs or second-hand clothing. **Though uniforms won't change their socioeconomic status, and though they still won't be able to afford the kinds of shoes and accessories that wealthier children sport, uniforms will enable them to feel significantly more comfortable among their peers.**

▶ In Short

Strong deductive arguments meet the following criteria:

- The conclusion and premises are clear and complete.
- The conclusion and premises are free of excessive subtle persuasion.
- The premises are credible and reasonable.
- The premises are sufficient and substantive.
- The argument considers the other side.

The more of these criteria your arguments meet, the more convincing you'll be.

Skill Building until Next Time

- Practice building your argument skills by playing devil's advocate. When you hear a deductive argument, think about what someone taking the opposite position might argue.
- When you hear or make an argument today, try to add more support to that argument. Add another major premise or add minor premises to support the major premises.

10 ▶ Putting It All Together

LESSON SUMMARY

This lesson puts together the strategies and skills you learned in Lessons 1–9. You'll review the key points of each lesson and practice evaluating claims and arguments.

Before going any further, it's time to review what you've learned in the preceding lessons so that you can combine strategies and put them to practical use. Repetition will help solidify ideas about what makes a good argument. Let's go through each lesson one at a time.

▶ Lesson 1: Critical Thinking and Reasoning Skills

You learned that critical thinking means carefully considering a problem, claim, question, or situation in order to determine the best solution. You also learned that reasoning skills involve using good sense and basing reasons for doing things on facts, evidence, or logical conclusions. Finally, you learned that critical thinking and reasoning skills will help you compose strong arguments, assess the validity of other people's arguments, make more effective and logical decisions, and solve problems and puzzles more efficiently and effectively.

▶ Lesson 2: Problem-Solving Strategies

You learned that the first step in solving any problem is to clearly identify the main issue and then break the problem down into its various parts. Next, you need to prioritize the issues and make sure that they're all relevant.

▶ Lesson 3: Thinking vs. Knowing

You practiced distinguishing between fact and opinion. Facts are things known for certain to have happened, to be true, or to exist. Opinions are things *believed* to have happened, to be true, or to exist. Tentative truths are claims that are thought to be facts but that need to be verified.

▶ Lesson 4: Who Makes the Claim?

You learned how to evaluate the credibility of a claim by learning how to recognize bias and determine the level of expertise of a source. You also learned why eyewitnesses aren't always credible.

▶ Lesson 5: Partial Claims and Half-Truths

You practiced identifying incomplete claims like those in advertisements. You also learned how averages can be misleading.

▶ Lesson 6: What's in a Word?

You learned how euphemisms, dysphemisms, and biased questions can be used to get people to react in a certain way. Euphemisms replace negative expressions with positive ones; dysphemisms replace neutral or positive expressions with negative ones; and biased questions make it difficult for you to answer questions fairly.

▶ Lesson 7: Working with Arguments

You learned that deductive arguments move from a conclusion to supporting evidence, or premises. You practiced identifying the conclusion and learned the difference between premises that provide separate support and those that are part of a chain of support.

▶ Lesson 8: Evaluating Evidence

You practiced looking carefully at evidence to determine whether or not it is valid. The two key criteria you analyzed were credibility and reasonableness.

▶ Lesson 9: Recognizing a Good Argument

Finally, you learned what makes a good argument: a conclusion and premises that are clear, complete, and free of excessive subtle persuasion; premises that are credible, reasonable, sufficient, and substantive; and a consideration of the other side.

> If any of these terms or strategies sound unfamiliar to you, STOP. Take a few minutes to review whatever lessons remain unclear.

Practice

You are on a crowded bus headed downtown. A burly, angry-looking teenager has just demanded that you give up your seat for him.

1. What is the main problem or issue?

2. What are the parts of the problem?

3. Consider the priority of these issues. What part of the problem should you address first? Second?

Answers

1. The main problem is deciding whether or not to give him your seat.

2. There are several issues here, including the following:
   - Could you be in danger if you refuse?
   - Will you be embarrassed if you give him your seat?
   - How should you tell him *no* if you decide to refuse?
   - Will others around you come to your aid if you refuse and he gets violent?
   - Are there any open seats on the bus? If so, then he may be looking for a fight.
   - How soon will you be getting off the bus?
   - Could he be ill? How can you tell?
   - How are you feeling? Do you need to sit down?
   - Do you notice anything about him to suggest that he may be violent?

3. The first issue you should probably address is your safety. In order to assess whether or not you are in danger if you refuse, there are other issues you'll have to address, including whether or not it appears that he's looking for a fight and whether or not you notice any signs that he may be violent. After you assess the level of danger, then you can consider other factors. If, for example, it looks like a refusal will result in trouble, are there other seats you could move to? Can you simply get off the bus at the next stop?

Practice

The following is a brief deductive argument. Read it carefully and then answer the questions that follow. The sentences are lettered to make the answers easier to follow.

(a) People are always complaining about the lack of funding for arts programs in schools. (b) I, however, do not think that this is as big a problem as people make it out to be. (c) In fact, I think that we should concentrate our spending on school programs that are meaningful, such as biology, reading, and math, not on ones that are useless, such as art and music appreciation. (d) Let's face it: The miracles that saints like doctors perform are more important. (e) Furthermore, an artist makes an average of $20,000 a year, whereas a doctor makes around $300,000 a year. (f) So, there is no doubt about it; we should spend money on textbooks, not on easels. (g) In the end, who do you think contributes to society more—the beatnik who paints all day or the scientist like me who spends his time in a lab finding the cure for cancer?

4. Underline any opinions you find in this passage.

5. Put brackets [ ] around any claims that you feel are tentative truths.

6. Are there any incomplete claims in this argument?

7. Evaluate the use of the word *average* in this passage. Is it acceptable?

8. Highlight any euphemisms, dysphemisms, or biased questions.

9. What is the conclusion of this argument?

10. What are the premises that support that conclusion?

11. Evaluate the premises. Are they credible? Reasonable?

12. Would you say that this is a good argument? Why or why not?

Answers

For answers to **4**, **5**, and **8**, opinions are underlined, tentative truths are bracketed, and persuasive techniques (such as euphemisms, dysphemisms, or biased questions) are in bold.

People are always complaining about the lack of funding for arts programs in schools. <u>I, however, do not think that this is as big a problem as people make it out to be. In fact, I think that we should concentrate our spending on school programs that are meaningful, such as biology, reading, and math, not on ones that are **useless**, such as art and music appreciation. Let's face it: The miracles that **saints like doctors perform** are more important.</u> [Furthermore, an artist makes an average of $20,000 a year, whereas a doctor makes around $300,000 a year.] <u>So, there is no doubt about it; we should spend money on textbooks, not on easels.</u> **In the end, who do you think contributes to society more—the beatnik who paints all day or the scientist like me who spends his time in a lab finding the cure for cancer?**

6. Yes. The arguer says, "Let's face it: The miracles that saints like doctors perform are more important." More important than what? The implied comparison is to artists, but the claim doesn't state that for sure.

7. Yes and no. The average salary given for artists may not be entirely accurate. For instance, does that statistic take into account highly successful artists like Philip Rothko or Picasso?

9. The conclusion is sentence **c**: "In fact, I think that we should concentrate our spending on school programs that are meaningful, such as biology, reading, and math, not on ones that are useless, such as art and music appreciation."

10. The premises that support the conclusion include sentences **d**, **e**, and **f**.

11. The premises in this argument are not very strong. Sentence **d**, for example, makes an incomplete claim, so it cannot be used as evidence to effectively support the claim. Sentence **e** can be accepted only as a tentative truth—the arguer doesn't cite his sources for the statistics that he provides; and sentence **f** is an opinion.

12. Overall, this is a poor argument. Most of the premises are either incomplete, biased, tentative truths, or opinions that are not supported with facts. Furthermore, the credibility of the arguer should be called into question. He stated that he is a scientist, so most likely, he is offering a biased perspective.

Skill Building until Next Time

- Review the "Skill Building" sections from each lesson in the past two weeks. Try any that you didn't do.
- Write a letter to a friend explaining what you've learned in the last ten lessons.

11 ▶ Logical Fallacies: Appeals to Emotion

LESSON SUMMARY

Arguments that appeal to people's emotions rather than to their sense of logic and reason abound in everyday life. In this lesson, you'll learn how to recognize several common appeals to emotion so that you can make more informed and logical decisions.

One of your coworkers, Ronald, is running for union representative. You've known him for several years. Ronald is good friends with your supervisor, Shawn, so you see him often—and you don't like what you see. You've seen Ronald treat other coworkers unfairly and talk rudely behind people's backs. You've decided to support another candidate who has always impressed you with her work ethic and generosity. But the day before the election, Ronald says to you, "I know I can count on your vote on Tuesday. After all, I know how much your job means to you. And you know that Shawn and I go back a long way." Even though you are on the committee that set up the voting procedure and voting booths, even though you know that it's almost impossible for Ronald to determine how you voted, and even though you're sure Shawn values you too much to fire you over your vote, you still vote for Ronald. Why? How did he get your vote?

It's probably not hard to see that Ronald took advantage of your desire to protect your well-being. Though you know better, he still made you think that your job was in jeopardy if you didn't vote for him. He got your vote not by arguing with any *reason* or *logic,* but by manipulating your *emotions.*

There are many strategies people will use to try to convince you that their conclusions are sound. Unfortunately, many of these strategies *appear* to be logical when, in fact, they're not. These strategies—often called **logical fallacies** or **pseudoreasoning** (false reasoning)—can lead you to make poor decisions and accept arguments that really don't hold water. That's why the next three lessons go over some of the most common logical fallacies. The more of them you can recognize—and the more you can avoid them in your own arguments—the better problem solver and decision-maker you will be.

This lesson addresses four fallacies that appeal to your emotions rather than to your sense of reason: scare tactics, flattery, peer pressure, and appeals to pity.

▶ Scare Tactics

In the opening scenario, Ronald appealed to your emotion of fear. You voted for him out of fear that you might lose your job if you didn't. He used his relationship with your supervisor to frighten you into accepting his conclusion (that you should vote for him). He didn't provide you with any logical reasons for giving him your vote; instead, he played upon your emotions. He used a logical fallacy known as *scare tactics*.

Scare tactics are used very commonly in deductive arguments, and they can be quite powerful. Though sometimes scare tactics cross the line and can become very real threats to your physical or emotional well-being, in most cases, you're not in any real danger. Once you know what to look for, you can see right through scare tactics. For example, read the following argument:

> Support Governor Wilson, or your children will receive a poor public school education.

Sounds convincing, doesn't it? After all, who wants their children to receive a poor education? But is this a good argument? Notice that the only reason this argument gives you for supporting the conclusion is emotional. It aims to *frighten* you into supporting Governor Wilson. The argument would be much more powerful if it also provided a logical reason for your support.

Practice

Read the following arguments carefully. If the argument uses logic to support the conclusion, write an **L** in the blank. If the argument uses scare tactics, write an **S** in the blank.

_____ **1.** We'd better leave now. If we don't, we might miss the last train and we'll be stuck here all night.

_____ **2.** I really think it'd be a good idea to do whatever she asks. She's a pretty powerful person.

_____ **3.** I really think it's a good idea to do whatever he asks. I've seen him fire people who say *no* to him.

Answers

1. L. The reasons given appeal to common sense.

2. S. This argument suggests that she is a person who can hurt you if you don't do what she wants.

3. S. This item may have tricked you, because it seems like this reason could be logical. But just because the arguer has seen this person fire others doesn't provide you with logical reasons for doing "whatever he asks." Who knows—what he asks of you could be illegal or dangerous. Just like your coworker Ronald, this person is trying to scare you into doing what he wants.

▶ Flattery

They say flattery will get you nowhere, but they're wrong. Flattery is powerful. So powerful, in fact, that it often leads people to make poor decisions and to accept arguments that really have no logical basis. Just as people can appeal to the sense of fear, they can also appeal to our **vanity,** which is another logical fallacy. Here's an example:

> You're a good citizen. You care about the future. That's why we know we can count on you to reelect Senator Houseman.

Notice how this argument doesn't give you any logical reasons for reelecting Senator Houseman. Instead, it flatters you; you like hearing that you're a good citizen and someone who cares about the future. While this may be true about you, is that any reason to reelect the senator? Not without evidence that he's done a good job during his first term. This argument doesn't give any evidence of his job performance.

Here's another example of an appeal to vanity:

> "Professor Wilkins, this is the best class I've ever taken. I'm learning so much from you! Thank you. By the way, I know that I missed an exam last week and that you normally don't let students make up missed exams. However, since you are such an excellent teacher, I thought you'd allow me to make up the test."

Here, the student doesn't give the teacher any reason to make an exception to her no-make-up policy. She may indeed be an excellent teacher and the student may indeed be learning a lot from her, but he's not giving her any good reasons; he's just buttering her up to get her to say yes.

Practice

Read the following arguments carefully. Are they using logic (**L**) or appealing to vanity (**V**)?

_____ **4.** Teacher to class: "This has been the best class I've ever taught. You're always so prepared and eager to learn! Thank you all so much. Now, I have these end-of-the-semester evaluations I need you to fill out. I know you'll all be honest and fill them out carefully. Thank you."

_____ **5.** "Claire, I'd like you to handle this typing project. You're the fastest typist and the best at reading my handwriting."

_____ **6.** "Claire, I know you don't mind a little extra work—you're such a good sport! So I'd like you to handle this typing project. You're the best. By the way, that's a terrific outfit."

Answers

4. V. This is a definite appeal to the students' vanity. The teacher is hoping that by buttering the students up a bit—telling them how wonderful they are—they'll be more generous in their evaluations of the class.

5. L. The speaker provides two logical, practical reasons for Claire to handle the project.

6. V. The speaker is trying to convince Claire she should do the extra work by flattering her. Notice that none of the reasons directly relates to her ability to do the work well.

▶ Peer Pressure

Along with fear and vanity, another extremely powerful emotion is our desire to be accepted by others. For example, children often do things they know are wrong because of pressure from friends. Unfortunately, many people continue to give in to peer pressure throughout their lives. **Peer pressure** is another form of false reasoning. It is an argument that says, "Accept the conclusion, or *you* won't be accepted." Take a look at the following arguments for examples of peer pressure:

> "C'mon, Sally. Stay. Everyone else is."

> "We're all voting *no*, Joe. You should, too."

In both these examples, the arguers don't offer any logical reasons for accepting their conclusions. Instead, they offer you acceptance—you'll be like everyone else. It's the old "everyone else is doing it" argument. The counterargument is exactly the one your mother gave you: If everyone else were jumping off a cliff, would you do it, too?

No one likes to be left out, and that's why we often give in to peer pressure. It *is* hard to be different and stand alone. But it is important to remember that our desire to belong is *not* a logical reason for accepting an argument. *Why* should Joe vote *no?* He needs to hear some specific, logical reasons. Otherwise, he's just falling victim to false logic.

Practice

Read the following arguments carefully. Are the arguers using logic (**L**) or peer pressure (**P**) to try to convince you?

_____ **7.** *"We* all think that the death penalty is the only way to cure society of rampant crime. Don't you?"

_____ **8.** "Come on, we're all voting for the Democrat again, just like the last time."

_____ **9.** "Stick with your party, Joe. The more unified we are, the more likely our candidates will win."

_____ **10.** "You should stop eating red meat. We've stopped and we feel much healthier."

Answers

7. P. The speaker tries to get you to agree by stressing that everyone else thinks that way. He suggests that if you disagree, you'll be alone in your belief.

8. P. Again, the speaker is using peer pressure. Here, the suggestion is that everyone else is voting the same way, so you should, too. But the speaker doesn't provide any logical reasons for voting for the Democrat.

9. L. This time, the speaker gives Joe a good logical reason for voting along the party line: Their party's candidates will win.

10. L. The speaker gives a good reason for considering his or her claim: They feel much better since they've stopped eating red meat. Of course, you'd probably want to hear more supporting arguments before you decide, but this argument doesn't try to sway you with emotion.

▶ Pity

Ms. Riviera, an eighth-grade history teacher, finds one of her students wandering the halls when she should be in class. The student tells the teacher, "I'm sorry, Ms. Riviera. I didn't realize I was out here so long. I'm just really upset about my math exam. I studied really hard for it and I only got a D on it. That means I'm going to be kicked off the tennis team!"

What should Ms. Riviera do?
a. Suspend the student. She should know better than this.
b. Send the student to the principal's office.
c. Take the student back to class and just give her a warning.
d. Call the student's parents and then expel the student.

Clearly, options **a** and **d** are unreasonable. But should Ms. Riviera give the student a break (choice **c**) just because she is upset? Is that a good enough reason for Ms. Riviera not to follow appropriate procedures, when the student clearly broke school rules?

Whether or not the student is telling the truth (and that's something Ms. Riviera will have to determine), she has appealed to another one of the most powerful emotions—the sense of pity and compassion for others. No one wants to be seen as heartless or uncaring. And that's why the appeal to **pity**, another logical fallacy, often works.

Here's another example of an appeal to pity:

Think of all the people who can't afford healthcare. Imagine the physical and emotional anguish they endure, knowing that having insurance coverage is all that it would take to alleviate their illness or disease. Support healthcare reform—for their sake.

Notice that this argument asks the listener to support a cause purely for *emotional* reasons. It appeals to the sense of compassion for those without healthcare. While this may be a compelling argument—after all, these people do deserve compassion—it is not a *logical* one. It doesn't directly address *why* healthcare reform is a reasonable policy.

Of course, you will have to judge each situation individually. But just as with the other appeals to emotion, it's important to have some logical reasons to balance the emotional. Unfortunately, if decisions are made based purely on pity, they often come back to haunt you. There are some people in the world who will take advantage of your sense of compassion, so think carefully before you act on pity alone.

Practice

Read the following arguments carefully. Are they using logic (**L**) to convince you, or are they appealing to your sense of pity and compassion (**P**)?

_____**11.** "But you can't fire me, Mr. Watts. I have seven mouths to feed!"

_____**12.** "But you can't fire me, Mr. Watts. I'm the only one who knows how to repair the machine. Besides, I have seven mouths to feed!"

_____**13.** "I know I don't have any experience, but I really need this job. My mom is sick and I'm the only child old enough to work."

Answers

11. P. The only reason the speaker gives for not being fired is that he has a family to feed. He doesn't make any argument regarding his ability to perform his duties at work.

12. L. And a little pity. The employee offers a logical reason for not firing him as well as an emotional one.

13. P. However, as always, you need to consider each case individually. Maybe the job this person is applying for doesn't require much experience, or maybe the applicant is a quick study. In that case, it might be OK to be swayed a little by pity.

▶ In Short

Appeals to emotions, including fear, vanity, desire to belong, and pity, can be very powerful. It is important to recognize when an argument uses emotional appeals—especially when emotional appeals are the only kind of support the argument offers.

Skill Building until Next Time

- Listen carefully for emotional appeals throughout the day. If you like to watch television, you'll see that these appeals are very often used in sitcoms.
- Think about something that you want someone to do for you. Think of several good, logical reasons for that person to say *yes*. Then, think of four different emotional appeals—one from each category—that you might use if you didn't know better.

12 ▶ Logical Fallacies: The Impostors

LESSON SUMMARY

Some forms of logical fallacies are tougher to recognize than others because they *seem* logical. This lesson will help you spot several common fallacies, including *circular reasoning* and *two wrongs make a right*.

Either you're with us or you're against us. Which is it?" Have you ever been put on the spot like this before, where you were forced to decide between two contradictory options? Chances are you have. But chances are you also had more choices than you thought.

Logical fallacies come in many forms. The last lesson covered the false reasoning that appeals to your emotions rather than to your sense of logic. This lesson will examine four logical fallacies that are sometimes a little harder to detect because they don't appeal to your emotions. As a result, they may *seem* logical even though they aren't. These types of fallacies are called **impostors.** Four types will be covered in this lesson, including *no in-betweens, slippery slope, circular reasoning,* and *two wrongs make a right.*

▶ No In-Betweens

No in-betweens (also called *false dilemma*) is a logical fallacy that aims to convince you that there are only two choices: X and Y, and nothing in between. The "logic" behind this fallacy is that if you think there are only two choices, then you won't stop to consider other possibilities. The arguer hopes that you will therefore be more likely to accept his or her conclusion.

For example, imagine that a husband and wife are planning a vacation to Hawaii. The husband says to his wife, "Either we stay for a whole week or we don't go at all." He gives no good reason for the seven-day minimum he is imposing, and it's obvious that he's using the no in-betweens tactic. By presenting his wife with only these two extremes, he forces her into the decision he wants. How could someone say *no* to a week in Hawaii when the alternative is no time at all in Hawaii?

It is important to remember that there are very few situations in which there are only two options. There are almost always other choices.

Practice

1. Read the following scenario. What other options are available?

Either you're a Republican or a Democrat. There's nothing in between.

Answer

There are plenty of other options. You could be independent (not registered with any party); you could be a member of the Independent Party; you could be a member of the Green Party; and so on. You could also be a Democrat but vote Republican on some issues, and vice versa. In other words, there are plenty of in-betweens here.

Practice

Read the following arguments carefully. Do the arguers use logic (L) or no in-betweens (NI) to convince you?

_____ **2.** Mother to son: "Either you major in engineering or in premed. Nothing else will lead to a good career."

_____ **3.** We can go to the movies or to the bowling alley. Unfortunately, because of the holiday, everything else is closed.

_____ **4.** Either we raise taxes by 10% or we drown ourselves in a budget deficit.

_____ **5.** Either you want to preserve our rainforests or you don't. You can't have it both ways.

Answers

2. NI. Indeed, there are other majors that can lead to a good career.

3. L. If everything else is closed, then these really are the only two options available.

4. NI. There are definitely other choices. Raising taxes isn't necessarily the only way to fix the budget deficit. Similarly, not raising taxes doesn't necessarily mean drowning in deficit. There are other ways to address the deficit problem.

5. NI. You can be in between on this issue. For example, you may want to preserve the rainforests, yet feel that we should harvest any plants that have disease-fighting properties.

▶ Slippery Slope

If scientists are allowed to experiment with cloning humans, next thing you know, they'll be mass producing people on assembly lines.

Right?

Well, maybe. But probably not, and definitely not for certain. This type of logical fallacy—often called **slippery slope**—presents an if/then scenario. It argues that if *X* happens, then *Y* will follow. This "next thing you know" argument has one major flaw, however: *X* doesn't necessarily lead to *Y*. When you hear someone make a claim in this format, you need to use your critical thinking and reasoning skills. You need to carefully consider whether or not there's a logical relationship between *X* and *Y*.

If scientists were to experiment with cloning human beings, for example, does that *necessarily* mean that humans would be mass produced on production lines? Definitely not. First of all, it may prove impossible to clone humans. Second, if it is possible, it's a long way from the production of a single clone to assembly-line production of clones. And third, if assembly-line cloning *is* possible, it may even be forbidden. So, though the thought of mass-produced human beings is frightening, it's not logical to restrict experiments because we're afraid of consequences that may not happen. More logical reasons need to be presented to justify limiting that kind of experimentation.

Practice

Read the following arguments carefully. Are they using logic (**L**) or slippery slope (**SS**) to convince you?

_____ **6.** If we raise the legal driving age to eighteen, then there will be less car accidents on the roads. People will feel safer on the road, and car insurance rates for everyone will decrease significantly.

_____ **7.** If all employers require their employees to take a flu shot, then less people would take sick days. This would result in increased productivity for the nation as a whole.

_____ **8.** I wouldn't drop this class if I were you. If you do, you'll be three credits behind and you'll have to take an extra class next semester to graduate on time.

Answers

6. SS. Raising the driving age to eighteen does not necessarily mean that there would be less car accidents on the roads. First of all, we can't be sure that the majority of car accidents that take place involve drivers under eighteen. Second, even if there were less car accidents as a result of the new driving age, it wouldn't necessarily result in lower insurance rates for everyone.

7. SS. Again, *X* doesn't necessarily lead to *Y*. There's no reason to believe that taking flu shots will increase productivity. Also, people can get sick for other reasons, and flu shots might not help in those cases.

8. L. This is a good, logical reason not to drop the class.

▶ Circular Reasoning

You're in a meeting when you decide to bring up what you think is an important issue. When you're finished, your boss turns to you and says, "Well, that's not important."

"Why not?" you ask.

"Because it just doesn't matter," he replies.

Your boss has just committed a very common logical fallacy called **circular reasoning** (also known as *begging the question*). Circular reasoning is a very appropriate name, because that's what this false logic does: It goes in a circle. Notice how your boss's argument doubles back on itself. In other words, his conclusion and premise say essentially the same thing:

Conclusion: That's not important.
Premise: It doesn't matter.

Instead of progressing logically from conclusion to evidence, the argument gets stuck at the conclusion. Like a dog chasing its tail, it goes nowhere. Here's another example:

You know that's not good for you; it isn't healthy.

Notice how the premise, "it isn't healthy," is no support for the conclusion, "that's not good for you"—rather, it simply restates it. Again, the argument goes nowhere.

Circular reasoning can be particularly tricky because a conclusion that doubles back on itself often *sounds* strong. That is, by restating the conclusion, you reinforce the idea that you're trying to convey. But you're *not* offering any logical reasons to accept that argument. When you hear someone make a claim that follows this format, look for a logical premise to support the conclusion—you probably won't find one.

Practice

See if you can recognize circular reasoning in the following arguments. If the argument is logical, write an **L** in the blank. If the argument is circular, write a **C** in the blank.

_____ **9.** I know he's telling the truth because he's not lying.

_____ **10.** He should have a break. He deserves it.

_____ **11.** Give him a break. He's been working nonstop for eight hours.

_____ **12.** It's the right thing to do, because this way, no one will get hurt.

_____ **13.** We believe this is the best choice because it's the right thing to do.

Answers

9. C. This argument doubles back on itself—"he's not lying" doesn't say any more than what's already been said in the conclusion.

10. C. Notice the premise doesn't give any reason for giving him a break. He "should have" one and "he deserves it" are the same thing.

11. L. The premise here offers a real reason. If he's been working "eight hours nonstop," he *does* deserve it.

12. L. Preventing people from getting hurt is a good supporting premise for the conclusion here.

13. C. Unlike number 12, the premise and the conclusion here say essentially the same thing.

▶ Two Wrongs Make a Right

Your friend has been having problems with her boyfriend. "What happened?" you ask.

"Well, he found out I went to Marco's party without him," she replies.

"Why did you do that?"

"He told Mary that he might go to Josie's party without me. So why can't I go to a party without him?"

It's time to have a talk with your friend. What she's saying here may *seem* to be logical, but, as with the other fallacies, it's not—the conclusion she draws doesn't come from good reasoning. Your friend has fallen victim to the two wrongs make a right fallacy.

The **two wrongs make a right** fallacy assumes that it's OK for you to do something to someone else because someone else *might* do that same thing to you. But two wrongs *don't* make a right, especially when you're talking about *mights*. If your friend's boyfriend *might* go to the party without her, does that make it okay for her to go to the party without him? Of course not.

Don't get this fallacy confused with the *eye for an eye* mentality. The *two wrongs* logical fallacy is not about getting even. It's about getting an edge. In an eye for an eye, you do something to someone because that person has *already* done it to you. But two wrongs make a right argues that you can do something simply because someone else *might* do it to you. And that's neither logical nor fair.

To show you how illogical this fallacy is, imagine the following scenario. You are walking home alone late at night. As you turn onto your street, you notice a man walking toward you. Although he gives no indication that he has any bad intentions, you clutch the canister of mace in your pocket. Just as you are about to cross paths, you decide—just to be on the safe side—to spray this stranger in the eyes. After all, you think, "What if he was planning to mug me? I better get him first."

As you can see, this approach is neither logical nor fair. It can also create a dangerous situation out of a perfectly normal one. Two wrongs that are built on a *maybe*—even a *probably*—don't make a right.

Practice

14. Put a check mark next to the arguments below that use the two wrongs make a right fallacy.

    a. Go ahead, tell your boss what you saw Edgar do. You know he'd report you in a second if he ever saw you do something like that.

    b. I agree with you, Paula. Since Maria didn't call you on your birthday, I don't think you should call her on her birthday either.

    c. John wants the job as badly as I do, so he'll probably start rumors about me to ruin my reputation. I'd better ruin his first.

Answers

Arguments **a** and **c** use the two wrongs make a right fallacy. Argument **b** may look like it does, but look again. In this case, the arguer is saying that Paula shouldn't call Maria on her birthday because Maria didn't call Paula on hers. This is truly an eye for an eye, not an eye for a maybe.

▶ In Short

Logical fallacies can appear to be logical; to avoid falling into their traps, you need to be on the lookout for false reasoning. The **no in-betweens** fallacy tries to convince you that there are only two choices when in reality, there are many options. The **slippery slope** fallacy tries to convince you that if you do X, then Y will follow—but in reality, X doesn't necessarily lead to Y. **Circular reasoning** is an argument that goes in a circle—the conclusion and premise say essentially the same thing. Finally, **two wrongs make a right** claims that it is OK to do something to someone else because someone else might do that same thing to you.

Skill Building until Next Time

- Each of the logical fallacies discussed in this lesson is very common. Listen for them throughout the day. Again, these fallacies are the kind you might see in various sitcoms, so look for them even when you're watching television.
- Think about something that you want someone to do for you. Come up with reasons based on the logical fallacies you learned in this lesson for that person to say yes. Then think of several good, logical reasons. Those are the reasons you should use when trying to convince someone of something.

13 ▶ Logical Fallacies: Distracters and Distorters

LESSON SUMMARY

In this final lesson about logical fallacies in deductive reasoning, you'll learn about fallacies that try to divert your attention from the main issue or to distort the issue so you're more likely to accept the argument. These fallacies include *ad hominem,* the *red herring,* and the *straw man.*

Imagine the following scenario: You have been renting your apartment for one year, and your landlord tells you that she is going to raise the rent $500 a month. One day, you run into another building tenant, Tina, in the hall. You tell her of your problem with the landlord. Tina gives you some advice. Later that week, you run into another tenant, Frank, who has heard about your predicament from Tina. Frank says to you, "Listen, I know this is none of my business, but if I were you, I wouldn't take Tina's advice about housing issues. She was evicted from her last apartment!"

Should you listen to Frank and ignore Tina's advice?

Since you haven't lived in the building for very long and don't know your neighbors very well, you have somewhat of a dilemma on your hands. Who do you trust? Who is more credible? You can't answer these questions because you are a fairly new tenant, but it is important that you realize that Frank has committed a logical fallacy. In this last lesson about logical fallacies in deductive reasoning, you'll learn about **distracters** and **distorters**— fallacies that aim to confuse the issues so that you more easily accept the conclusion of the argument. *Ad hominem* will be discussed first, followed by red herrings and the straw man.

▶ Ad Hominem

What has Frank done wrong? Indeed, since Tina was evicted from her last apartment, how *can* she give you good advice? It would appear as if what Frank says makes a lot of sense.

Frank's argument may seem logical, but it's not. That's because Frank is not attacking Tina's *advice*; instead, he's simply attacking *Tina*. This kind of false reasoning is called **ad hominem**, which in Latin means, "to the man." *Ad hominem* fallacies attack the *person* making the claim rather than the *claim* itself.

An *ad hominem* fallacy can take a variety of forms. You can attack a person, as Frank does, for his or her personality or actions. You can also attack a person for his or her beliefs or affiliations. For example, you might say, "Don't listen to him. He's a liberal." Or you can attack a person for his or her nationality, ethnicity, appearance, occupation, or any other categorization. For example, imagine someone says to you:

"Of course he's wrong. Someone who dresses like that obviously doesn't have a clue about anything."

This is a clear-cut case of *ad hominem*.

Ad hominem aims to distract you from looking at the validity of the claim by destroying the credibility of the person making the claim. But the trouble with *ad hominem* is that it doesn't really take into account the issue of credibility. Just because Tina was evicted from her last apartment doesn't mean she can't give you good advice about how to deal with your landlord. In fact, because she's dealt with a fairly serious housing issue, she might be considered more of an expert than most. It all depends on what kind of advice you're looking for. Maybe Tina was a victim of circumstance. Whatever the case, Tina may still be in a position to give you good advice. If Frank wants to prove his point, he needs to attack Tina's actual *argument* about how to handle your landlord rather than to attack Tina herself.

To clarify when something is and isn't an *ad hominem*, read the following example:

A. Don't listen to what Bob says about investments. That guy is the most money-grubbing creep I've ever met.
B. I wouldn't listen to what Bob says about investments if I were you. He recently made his own investment decisions and lost all of his money in the stock market.

Are either of these *ad hominem* fallacies? Both? Neither?

You probably saw that argument A uses *ad hominem* quite shamelessly. So what if Bob is a "money-grubber"? That doesn't mean he can't have good advice about investments. In fact, if he's greedy, he may be quite knowledgeable about the kinds of investments that make the most money. Whether you *like* him or not is a separate matter from whether he has good advice or not. His "money-grubbing" nature should not really affect the credibility of his argument. Remember, credibility is based on freedom from bias and on expertise—not on appearance, personality, past behavior, or beliefs.

If, on the other hand, Bob has recently made investments and lost his money, his expertise in the matter of investments should be called into question. He has experience in investing, yes—but his experience shows that he may not be too knowledgeable about the subject. You should probably investigate further before deciding whether or not to listen to his advice. At any rate, at least argument B avoids the *ad hominem* fallacy.

Ad hominem fallacies can also work in reverse. That is, the argument can urge you to *accept* someone's argument based on who or what the person is rather than on the validity of the premises. For example:

Len says, "I agree with Rich. After all, he's a Lithuanian, too."

Does the fact that Len and Rich share the same nationality mean that Rich's argument—whatever it may be—is valid? Of course not.

Practice

Read the arguments below carefully. Do they use the *ad hominem* fallacy?

1. Well, if that's what Harvey said, then it must be true.

2. Well, he's got twenty years of experience dealing with consumer complaints, so I think we should trust his advice.

3. He's good, but he's just not right for the job. After all, he's a Jets fan!

4. Manager A to manager B: "I know we need to address the problem. But Caryn doesn't know what she's talking about. She's just a secretary."

Answers

1. **Yes.**
2. **No.** His experience makes him credible, and that's a good reason to trust his advice.
3. **Yes.**
4. **Yes.** Just because she's a secretary and not a manager doesn't mean she doesn't have a good perspective on the problem. In fact, because she's "in the trenches," Caryn's ideas are probably very valuable to the managers.

▶ Red Herring

Just what is a **red herring?** Strange name for a logical fallacy, isn't it? But the name makes sense. Cured red herrings were previously used to throw dogs off the track of an animal they were chasing. And that's exactly what a *red herring* does in an argument: It takes you off the track of the argument by bringing in an unrelated topic to divert your attention from the real issue. Here's an example:

Making English the official language of this country is wrong, and that's part of the problem here. A country can't claim to be a "melting pot" when it doesn't try to reach out to all nationalities.

First, break down the argument. What's the conclusion?

Conclusion: Making English the official language is wrong.

Now, what are the premises?

Premises:
1. That's part of the problem here.
2. A country can't claim to be a "melting pot" when it doesn't try to reach out to all nationalities.

Do the premises have anything to do with the conclusion? In fact, do these premises have anything to do with each other? No. Instead of supporting the conclusion, the premises aim to sidetrack you by bringing up at least three different issues:

1. What's part of the problem here.
2. What makes a "melting pot."
3. Why the country doesn't reach out to all nationalities.

Red herrings like these can be so distracting that you forget to look for support for the conclusion that the arguer presents. Instead of wondering why making English the official language is wrong, you may be wondering what *does* make a "melting pot" or why the country *doesn't* reach out to all nationalities—that is, if you accept the claim that the country doesn't reach out to all nationalities.

Red herrings are a favorite of politicians and people who want to turn potential negative attention away from them and onto others. Watch how it works:

> **Senator Wolf:** "Yes, I support Social Security reform. I know that Senator Fox is against it, but he's just trying to get the liberal vote."

Notice how Senator Wolf avoids having to explain or defend his position by shifting the attention away from his claim and onto Senator Fox. Instead of supporting his claim, he leaves the listener wondering if Senator Fox is just out to get more votes. Once again, the red herring tactic throws the argument off track.

Practice

Read the following arguments carefully. Do you see any red herrings? If so, underline them.

5. Yes, I believe that it is time for rent laws to change, and here's why. It's very hard to pay my rent since my income is so low. How would you feel if you worked forty hours a week and could barely make ends meet? It's time for a change!

6. It is wrong to censor the press. Our government has a law in the First Amendment that allows the press to express itself without interference or constraint by the government.

7. Do you want to know why there are some people without healthcare? It's because too many politicians don't want to raise taxes because they are afraid they will lose votes.

8. You should become a vegetarian. After all, do you know how many animals are on the verge of extinction?

Answers

5. Yes, I believe that it is time for rent laws to change, and here's why. <u>It's very hard to pay my rent since my income is so low. How would you feel if you worked forty hours a week and could barely make ends meet? It's time for a change!</u>

6. It is wrong to censor the press. Our government has a law in the First Amendment that allows the press to express itself without interference or constraint by the government. (This argument provides relevant evidence for the conclusion.)

7. Do you want to know why there are some people without healthcare? <u>It's because too many politicians don't want to raise taxes because they are afraid they will lose votes.</u>

8. You should become a vegetarian. <u>After all, do you know how many animals are on the verge of extinction?</u> (True, vegetarians don't eat meat, but the kind of meat carnivores eat are not the animals that are on the verge of extinction. Instead of this red herring, this argument should give good reasons for giving up chicken, pork, beef, and the other types of meat common to the human diet.)

► Straw Man

Have you ever gotten in a fight with a scarecrow? It's pretty easy to win, isn't it, when you're fighting a man made of straw. After all, he's not a real man—he falls apart easily and he can't fight back. You're safe and your opponent is a goner. It probably doesn't surprise you that there's a logical fallacy that uses this principle: It sets up the opponent as a straw man, making it easy to knock him down.

Specifically, the **straw man** fallacy takes the opponent's position and distorts it. The position can be oversimplified, exaggerated, or otherwise misrepresented. For example, if someone were arguing *against* tax reform, he or she might distort the reformers' position by saying:

> "The people who support tax reform are only out to get a break in their own capital gains taxes."

Even if getting a tax break is one of the reasons people support tax reform, it can't be the only one—after all, tax reform is a pretty complicated issue. Furthermore, the arguer, using the straw man tactic, presents the reformers as selfish and greedy—in it only for themselves—which makes it easier for the listeners not to want to support their position.

Similarly, if someone were arguing *for* tax reform, he or she might set up a straw man like the following:

> "The folks who oppose tax reform simply don't want to go to the trouble of restructuring the IRS."

True, restructuring the IRS may be one concern of the opponents, but is it their main concern? Is that the real reason they don't support it? Chances are, their opposition stems from a number of issues, of which reforming the IRS is only one. Once again, the straw man has misrepresented and oversimplified, making the opponent easy to knock down. In both cases, the reasons for support or opposition are difficult to approve of. One argument claims that the supporters are selfish and the other claims that the opponents are protecting the bureaucracy of the IRS—and neither of these is an admirable position.

Straw men are very commonly used in arguments because people often don't take the time to consider all sides of an issue or because they don't have the courage or counterarguments to address the complete issue. For example, imagine that someone says:

> "Those environmentalists! They're all trying to make us spend more money on electric automobiles instead of letting us continue to drive gas-powered ones."

Clearly, this is a misinterpreted "definition" of environmentalists. Indeed, it's difficult to sum up what environmentalists—or any group—believe in just one sentence. But if you present environmentalists this way, it becomes very easy to avoid coming up with effective counterarguments, and it certainly becomes difficult to say that environmentalism is a positive thing.

The trouble is, how do you know if you're being presented with a straw man? What if you've never studied environmentalism or don't know much about the environmentalist movement? What if you haven't paid much attention to the news about tax reform? In short, how do you know when an opponent is being misrepresented?

Your best bet is to be as informed and educated as possible. And you can do that by reading and listening as much as possible. Watch the news, read the paper, listen to the radio, read magazines—pay attention to things like politics and social issues. The more informed you are, the better you'll be able to see if and when someone is trying to "pull the wool over your eyes" with a straw man.

Practice

Do any of the following arguments use a straw man?

9. All the union members want is to put us middle managers out of work.

10. Lawyers don't really care about helping people. They're just out to make as much money as they can.

11. LeeAnne feels that it's unwise for managers to have their own lounge because it reduces interaction with other employees and limits opportunities for spontaneous learning.

Answers

9. Yes. The middle managers misrepresent the position of the union members.

10. Yes. This argument makes a sweeping generalization that misrepresents the position of all lawyers.

11. No. This argument makes sense—LeeAnne's position is specific and clear.

▶ In Short

Now you're armed with three more fallacies to watch out for: *ad hominem*, the **red herring**, and the **straw man**. In *ad hominem*, the arguer attacks the *person* instead of the claim. A red herring brings in an irrelevant issue to throw the argument off track. The straw man presents a distorted picture of the opponent so that the opponent will be easy to knock down. Be on the lookout for these and the other fallacies you've learned as you check for the validity of arguments.

Skill Building until Next Time

- One way to help you recognize these fallacies is to be sure you can commit them yourself. So, like you did in the previous two lessons, think of several good, logical reasons to support an argument. Then, come up with examples of each of the logical fallacies you learned in this lesson.
- Listen to a call-in talk show on the radio or watch a debate on television, preferably one where audience members are allowed to participate. Listen carefully for the logical fallacies that you've learned. Chances are, you'll catch a lot of people trying to get away with false logic.

14 ▶ Why Did It Happen?

LESSON SUMMARY

In this lesson, you'll learn how explanations are different from arguments. You'll also learn the criteria for determining whether the explanation you're being offered is good or not.

Y ou are an hour and a half late to work. The moment you walk through the door, your boss calls you into his office. "Where have you been?" he asks. "I demand an explanation."

Explanations are very closely related to arguments, but they're not quite the same thing. Whereas an argument generally aims to convince you that a certain claim is true, an explanation aims to convince you *why* a claim is true. For example, compare the following examples:

1. You should be more careful going down these stairs. They're steep and lots of people fall.
2. He fell down the stairs because they're very steep and he wasn't careful.

The first example is an argument. The writer is trying to convince you to be more careful on the stairs (conclusion) because the steps are steep (premise) and lots of people fall (premise). The second example, on the other hand, is an explanation. The writer here is telling you *why* someone fell down the stairs—because they're steep and because he wasn't careful.

So explanations are different from arguments. But what does this have to do with critical thinking and reasoning skills?

Well, just as you will be presented with arguments of all types almost every day of your life, you will also be presented with explanations of all kinds. And just as you need to evaluate arguments carefully before you decide whether or not to accept them, you should also evaluate explanations carefully before you decide whether or not they're valid.

When it comes to explanations, there are four criteria that you should look for:

1. Relevance
2. Testability
3. Circularity
4. Compatibility with existing knowledge

▶ Relevance

One of the first tests any explanation should undergo is the test for **relevance.** Is the explanation that is provided clearly relevant to the issue being explained? That is, is there a clear and obvious connection between the issue and the explanation?

For example, you might say to your boss, "I'm late because the electricity went off during the night and my alarm never went off." Is that relevant? Absolutely. Your ability to arrive on time depends upon your ability to wake up on time. However, an explanation like the following is certainly *not* relevant:

"I'm late because Macy's is having a sale this weekend."

Macy's sale—while it may be important to you—has no bearing on your ability to get to work on time. This is obvious, of course, but that doesn't prevent people from offering irrelevant explanations.

Practice

1. Provide another relevant and another irrelevant reason for being late to work.

Relevant:

Irrelevant:

Answers

1. Answers will vary. You might have written something like the following:

Relevant: My car broke down and I had to wait an hour for the tow truck.
Irrelevant: I need a new car radio.

One important thing to keep in mind about explanations is that an explanation can pass the relevancy test and still not be a *good* explanation. For example, "I'm late because last night I was at a Super-Bowl party" is not a *good* explanation, but it is a *relevant* explanation—because you were out late, you didn't get up in time for work.

Practice

Read the following explanations carefully. Are they relevant (**R**) or irrelevant (**I**)?

_____ **2.** I didn't go because it was snowing heavily outside.

_____ **3.** I didn't get accepted into the program because I didn't get my application in on time.

_____ **4.** I didn't make it to practice because my favorite shoe store was having a grand opening in my neighborhood.

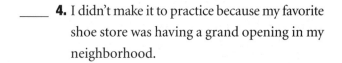

Answers

2. R. Bad weather is a relevant explanation for not going somewhere. Snow can affect the driving conditions and make it dangerous to go anywhere.

3. R. Not getting an application in by a deadline is a relevant explanation for failing to get accepted into a program.

4. I. The grand opening of a shoe store is not a relevant explanation for not making it to practice.

▶ Testability

You may not be a scientist, but you've certainly performed some experiments in your life. You may have bought different brands of detergent, for example, to see which brand got your clothes cleaner. Or you may have tried different cold medicines to see which worked best for you. This type of experimenting enables you to explain why you use the brand you use: "I use Rinse-All because it doesn't bother my sensitive skin," for example. This explanation is one that can be tested. It therefore passes the next test of validity for explanations: **testability**.

Testability is as important as relevance when it comes to evaluating explanations. If someone provides an explanation that is impossible to test, then you should be highly suspicious. An **untestable explanation** is one that is impossible to verify through experimentation. And that's precisely why you should be on guard.

For example, imagine that someone offers you the following explanation:

Global warming is caused by invisible, weightless particles being hurled at us from an invisible universe.

Is there any way to test this explanation? If the particles can't be seen or weighed, and if the universe they come from is invisible, then no one can prove that this is or *isn't* the cause. It can't be verified and it can't be refuted. The theory is untestable (and absurd, but that's another story).

Here's another example:

We met because we were meant to meet.

Is there any way to test this explanation? No. There's no test for fate, after all. Though it may be romantic, this is an untestable—and therefore invalid—explanation.

Practice

Read the following explanations carefully. Are they testable (**T**) or untestable (**U**)?

_____ **5.** You won the competition because it was in the stars.

_____ **6.** I got the job because I had all the qualifications they were looking for.

_____ **6.** You were given that item because you no one else showed up to claim it.

_____ **7.** You didn't get hurt because luck was on your side.

Answers

5. U. There's no way to verify that something happened because it was "in the stars.

6. T. This can be verified. You can ask your employer why he or she chose you for the job.

7. T. This can be verified. You can find out if anyone else went to claim the item.

8. U. There's no way to verify if luck is ever on anyone's "side."

► Circularity

In Lesson 12, "Logical Fallacies: The Impostors," you learned about circular reasoning: arguments that double back on themselves because the conclusion and the premise say essentially the same thing. Explanations can be circular, too. You might say to your boss, for example:

> I'm late because I didn't get here on time.

That's a **circular explanation**. "I'm late" and "I didn't get here on time" say essentially the same thing. The "explanation" simply restates the situation rather than explains it, and that doesn't make for a valid explanation.

Here's another example:

> The inflation was caused by an increase in prices.

Notice that "inflation" and "increase in prices" are essentially the same thing. Once again, this is an explanation that goes in a circle. The explanation does not offer any insight as to how or why the situation occurred.

Practice

Read the explanations below carefully. Identify explanations that pass (**P**) the logic test and those that fail (**F**) because they are circular.

_____ **9.** He has insomnia because he has trouble sleeping.

_____ **10.** She's a genius because she's gifted.

_____ **11.** They work well together because they share the same goals.

_____ **12.** He keeps the birds in separate cages because he doesn't want to keep them together.

_____ **13.** He got sick because he didn't dress warmly enough.

Answers

9. F. "Insomnia" and "has trouble sleeping" are two ways of saying the same thing.

10. F. Being a genius and being gifted are just about the same, so there's no real explanation given here.

11. P. This explanation gives a reason that explains why they work well together.

12. F. A good explanation would tell why the birds can't be kept together.

13. P. This gives a reason for why he got sick.

More Practice

Write two circular explanations of your own on a separate sheet of paper. To see if they're really circular, use this test: Does the explanation (usually the part that comes after the word *because*) really express the same idea as the issue you're supposed to be explaining?

► Compatibility with Existing Knowledge

Your boss didn't like your "I'm late because I didn't get here on time" explanation, so you try again:

> "I'm late because my helicopter is in the shop and I had to find another way to get here."

Chances are, your boss won't find your explanation very amusing—and he definitely won't find it valid. Why? Because he knows that there's no way you get to work by helicopter. You get to work by car, bus, train, or some other means of transportation, but not by helicopter. Your explanation goes against what he knows to be true, so he has every right to be very suspicious of your explanation.

Scientific discoveries and technological breakthroughs often surprise people and sometimes shatter theories that were long thought to be true. Remember, people once believed that the Earth was flat. Still, in everyday life, it's a good idea to be wary of explanations that go against what you know from your past experience or from your education. For example, if you know that the office copier was just fixed this morning, and your assistant says she didn't finish the copies you requested because the copier is broken, you have good reason to doubt the validity of her explanation. Similarly, if your neighbor tells you that gravity is actually caused by a giant U-shaped magnet located at the center of the Earth, you should be highly suspicious since his explanation conflicts with accepted scientific theories about the makeup of the Earth's interior.

Some explanations, however, may sound odd or surprising to you without necessarily contradicting what you know from your experience or education. In this case, it's probably best to suspend your judgment anyway, until you can verify the explanation. Like *tentative truths,* these explanations might be valid, but you need to learn more before accepting them as true.

For example, imagine you are the boss and an employee tells you, "I'm late because there was a major accident on the freeway." Now you know that things like this happen. Depending upon the credibility of that employee, you could:

- Accept that explanation as fact
- Accept that explanation as a tentative truth
- Reject the explanation, especially if that employee has a history of lying

In a case like this, the credibility of the person offering the explanation is a key factor. But it's important to note that this is not an untestable explanation. You could listen to traffic reports on the radio, talk to other employees who take that freeway, or watch for a report of an accident in tonight's paper to find out if the employee was telling the truth.

Practice

Consider the following explanations and their sources. Are they acceptable? Why or why not?

14. Your long-time coworker and friend says: "I'm sorry I can't cover your shift tomorrow. I have a doctor's appointment and I can't reschedule again."

15. Your local garage mechanic says: "Your car broke down because your transmission is shot. It's going to need a lot of work."

16. Your neighbor says: "I don't exercise because it's bad for your health. It wears your body down."

Answers

14. If you've worked with this person a long time and consider her a friend, then this explanation is acceptable.

15. The acceptability of this explanation would depend partly upon how much you know about cars. A ruined transmission is a very costly repair. If you don't know much about cars and don't know your mechanic very well, it might do you good to get a second opinion.

16. Unacceptable. All evidence points to exercise as a key to improving health and living a longer life.

▶ In Short

Explanations, much like arguments, need to meet certain criteria before you should feel comfortable accepting them. To be valid, an explanation should be **relevant**—clearly related to the event or issue in question—and **testable**—able to be verified in some way. **Circular explanations**—ones that double back on themselves like circular arguments—should be rejected, and you should be careful about accepting explanations that contradict your knowledge or accepted theories.

Skill Building until Next Time

- Pay attention to the explanations around you: at home, at work, at school, and on TV. See how often you find people offering explanations that don't meet the criteria discussed in this lesson.
- Once again, sitcoms can help you sharpen your critical thinking and reasoning skills. Characters on sitcoms often find themselves in situations where they have to come up with a quick explanation—and usually those explanations are quite bad. Be on the lookout for these explanations and use the criteria you've learned to evaluate them. Are they relevant? Circular? Testable? Just plain absurd?

15 ▶ Inductive Reasoning

LESSON SUMMARY

In this lesson, you'll review the difference between deductive and inductive reasoning. You'll also sharpen your inductive reasoning skills by learning how to draw logical conclusions from evidence.

Lesson 7, "Working with Arguments," talked about the difference between inductive and deductive reasoning. In deductive reasoning, as you know, an argument moves from a conclusion to the evidence (premises) that supports that conclusion. **Inductive arguments,** on the other hand, move from evidence to a conclusion drawn from that evidence.

As a critical thinker, when you come across a deductive argument, you should examine the validity of the *evidence* for the conclusion. If the evidence is valid, the conclusion—and therefore the whole argument—is a good one. However, in inductive reasoning, the goal is not to test the validity of the evidence. Rather, it is to examine the validity of the *conclusion*. If the conclusion stems logically from the evidence, then the argument can be considered a good one.

But how do you know if the conclusion is logical? In inductive reasoning, the main criterion is to determine the **likelihood** that the premises lead to the conclusion. Likelihood can be judged based on:

1. Common sense
2. Past experience

Of course, formal logic, involving mathematical symbols, can also help, but that won't be discussed in this book.

Here's an example of a brief inductive argument:

Due to a storm, there was a major power-outage last night in a nearby town. A lot of people must have used flashlights and lit candles to see.

If the premise that there was a major power-outage in a nearby town is true, is it reasonable to assume that a lot of people lit candles and used flashlights to see? What do *you* think—is a power-outage at night likely to cause people to turn on flashlights and light candles? Based on common sense and past experience, you can say with confidence *yes*. Is it very likely? Again, you can confidently say *yes*. Therefore, this is a good inductive argument—a logical conclusion drawn from common sense and past experience; or substantial evidence.

▶ The Science of Inductive Reasoning

Any time someone draws conclusions from evidence, inductive reasoning is being used. Scientists use it all the time. For example, let's say a scientist takes two equally healthy plants of the same size, age, and type. She puts Plant A in a room with a radio that plays only classical music. She puts Plant B in a room with a radio that plays only rock and roll. Both plants receive equal light and water. After six weeks, Plant A has grown six inches. Plant B, on the other hand, has grown only three inches, which is the average growth rate for these types of plants. She repeats this experiment and gets the same results. Using her inductive reasoning skills, what is the most logical thing for the scientist to conclude?

    a. In both cases, Plant B must not have been as healthy to start as Plant A.
    b. Plants grow better when exposed to classical music than to rock and roll.
    c. Rock and roll music stunts plant growth.

Well, common sense would suggest that choice **a** isn't an option, because it is stated that both plants were equally healthy at the start of the experiment. Furthermore, since it is known that Plant B grew at the *normal* rate, then **c** can't be a logical conclusion either. But even without this process of elimination, common sense and the results of the two experiments point to conclusion **b,** that plants grow better to classical music than to rock and roll. (This is true, by the way!)

Of course, this conclusion would be even more valid if the scientist repeated the experiment several more times and continued to get the same results. The more she performs the experiment and gets the same results, the stronger her argument will be.

▶ Elementary, My Dear Watson

Detectives, like scientists, also use inductive reasoning. In the following excerpt from the story "The Reigate Puzzle," for example, the famous fictional character Sherlock Holmes uses inductive reasoning to solve a tricky crime. By examining a piece of a torn document, he is able to conclude that *two* different men wrote the document, and he's able to determine which of the two men is the "ringleader." Read how he does it:

"And now I made a very careful examination of the corner of paper which the Inspector had submitted to us. It was at once clear to me that it formed part of a very remarkable document. Here it is. Do you not now observe something very suggestive about it?" [said Holmes.]

"It has a very irregular look," said the Colonel.

"My dear sir," cried Holmes, "there cannot be the least doubt in the world that it has been written by two persons doing alternate words. When I draw your attention to the strong *t*'s of 'at' and 'to,' and ask you to compare them with the weak ones of 'quarter' and 'twelve,' you will instantly recognize the fact. A very brief analysis of these four words would enable you to say with the utmost confidence that the 'learn' and the 'maybe' are written in the stronger hand, and the 'what' in the weaker."

"By Jove, it's as clear as day!" cried the Colonel. "Why on earth should two men write a letter in such a fashion?"

"Obviously the business was a bad one, and one of the men who distrusted the other was determined that, whatever was done, each should have an equal hand in it. Now, of the two men, it is clear that the one who wrote the 'at' and 'to' was the ringleader."

"How do you get at that?"

"We might deduce it from the mere character of the one hand as compared with the other. But we have more assured reasons than that for supposing it. If you examine this scrap with attention you will come to the conclusion that the man with the stronger hand wrote all of his words first, leaving blanks for the other to fill up. These blanks were not always sufficient, and you can see that the second man had to squeeze to fit his 'quarter' in between the 'at' and the 'to,' showing that the latter were already written. The man who wrote all his words first is undoubtedly the man who planned the affair."

Notice how Holmes looks carefully at the document and uses what he sees to make logical inferences (draw logical conclusions) about the two men responsible for the crime. The difference in the t's indicates two different writers and the uneven spacing of the words indicates who wrote first, thus leading Holmes to conclude that the man who wrote first was the man "who planned the affair."

Practice

Now it is your turn to play detective and use your reasoning skills to draw logical inferences. Read carefully the information you are given (the premises) and consider what would be the most logical conclusion to draw from that evidence.

1. Every time it rains outside, your bad knee starts to ache. When you wake up this morning, you find that your bad knee is sore. You can therefore logically conclude
   a. today is going to be a clear, sunny day.
   b. it's going to rain today.
   c. there is a lot of humidity in the air.

2. Every September, you receive an envelope that contains a bonus check from your employer. Every November, your boss calls you into his office to tell you whether or not you're getting a raise this year. When you arrive to work on the morning of September 5, there is an envelope with your name on it lying on your desk. You can therefore logically conclude
   a. you are getting laid off.
   b. you are getting a raise.
   c the envelope contains your yearly bonus check.

3. The last two summers you went to the beach, you used "Sun-Off" sunblock with an SPF of 50. But both summers, you got a terrible sunburn. You can therefore logically conclude
   a. you need to use a sunblock with a higher SPF.
   b. you should wear pants and long sleeves when you go in the sun.
   c. "Sun-Off" sunblock might not be a very good product, and you should try another one next summer.

4. If you got a sunburn after using "Sun-Off" only one summer instead of two in a row, would you draw the same conclusion? Why or why not?

5. Whenever you eat something with cayenne pepper in it, you get an allergic reaction where you find it hard to breathe. You always ask the waiter or waitress in a restaurant to make sure the chef does not use any cayenne pepper in the dish you are ordering. Tonight, as you eat the dish you ordered, you begin to develop an allergic reaction. You can therefore logically conclude

   a. the waiter forgot to tell the chef not to put any cayenne pepper in your dish.

   b. the food was not refrigerated properly before it was cooked.

   c. you are allergic to something else.

Answers

1. It would be most logical to conclude choice **b**, that it is going to rain today. Choice **c** is another possibility, but because it always rains when your knee hurts, **b** is a more likely possibility.

2. The most logical choice is **c**, the envelope contains your yearly bonus check. Although choices **a** and **b** are always possibilities, you receive your raises in November and you have no reason to believe you're getting laid off, which makes these choices less likely than **c**.

3. Based on your last two experiences, the best choice is **c**. Choice **a** is improbable, as an SPF of 50 is the highest SPF available. Choice **b**, too, is unlikely, as a good sunblock should allow you to expose yourself to the sun without getting a sunburn.

4. If there were only one instance of getting a sunburn using "Sun-Off" sun block, you might not conclude the same thing. You might, for example, conclude that the sunblock washed off too quickly to work properly, or that you stayed in the sun too long. Whatever you suspect to be the cause of your sunburn, you most likely would give "Sun-Off" the benefit of the doubt the first time.

5. The most logical thing to conclude would be choice **a**. Choice **b** is unlikely—restaurants have health codes that they have to follow, and it is a rare occurrence that food is improperly refrigerated in a restaurant. Choice **c**, too, is unlikely. Although a possibility, it would not be the most logical conclusion to draw.

▶ In Short

Inductive reasoning is the process of drawing conclusions from evidence. A good inductive argument is one in which it is very likely that the premises lead to the conclusion. Past experience and common sense can be used to measure that likelihood.

Skill Building until Next Time

- Notice how often you use inductive reasoning throughout your day. At home, work, or school, as you travel from place to place, what conclusions do you draw from what you see around you?
- Read a detective story or watch a detective show like *Without a Trace, NYPD Blue,* or *Law & Order.* Pay special attention to how detectives use evidence to draw conclusions about the crime.

16 ▶ Jumping to Conclusions

LESSON SUMMARY

Just as there are logical fallacies to beware of in deductive reasoning, there are several logical fallacies to look out for in inductive reasoning. This lesson will show you how to recognize and avoid those fallacies.

Imagine a coworker of yours, Dennis, bumps into you during a coffee break. "You know, I tried the coffee at the new deli this morning," he says, "and it was lousy. What a shame, the new deli stinks."

Oops. Dennis has just been caught jumping to conclusions.

Inductive reasoning, as you know, is all about drawing conclusions from evidence. But sometimes, people draw conclusions that aren't quite logical. That is, conclusions are drawn too quickly or are based on the wrong kind of evidence. This lesson will introduce you to the three logical fallacies that lead to illogical conclusions in inductive reasoning: *hasty generalizations, biased generalizations,* and *non sequiturs.*

▶ Hasty Generalizations

A **hasty generalization** is a conclusion that is based on too little evidence. Dennis's conclusion about the new deli is a perfect example. He'd only been to the new deli once, and he'd only tried one item. Has he given the deli a fair chance? No. First of all, he's only tried the coffee, and he's only tried it one time. He needs to have the coffee a few more times before he can fairly determine whether or not their coffee is any good. Second, he needs to try their other foods as well before he can pass judgment on the whole establishment. Only after he has collected this "evidence" will he have enough premises to lead to a logical conclusion.

Here's another example of a hasty generalization. Let's say you're introduced to a woman named Ellen at work, and she barely acknowledges you. You decide she's cold and arrogant. Is your conclusion fair? Maybe Ellen was preoccupied. Maybe she was sick. Maybe she had a big meeting she was heading to. Who knows? The point is, you only met her once, and you drew a conclusion about her based on too little evidence.

A few weeks later, you meet Ellen again. This time, she's friendly. She remembers meeting you, and you have a pleasant conversation. Suddenly you have to revise your conclusion about her, don't you? Now you think she's nice. But the *next* time you see her, she doesn't even say hello. What's happening here? You keep jumping to conclusions about Ellen. But you really need to have a sufficient number of encounters with her before you can come to any conclusions.

Hasty generalizations have a lot in common with stereotypes. In the case of stereotypes, conclusions about an entire group are drawn based upon a small segment of that group. Likewise, hasty generalizations draw conclusions about something based on too small a sample, such as one cup of coffee, or two or three encounters with Ellen.

Here are a few more hasty generalizations:

Brandon is a jock, and he's a lousy student. All jocks are lousy students.

Suzie is blonde, and she has a lot of fun. So I guess it's true that blondes have more fun.

You'd need to see a lot more examples of jocks and blondes before either of these conclusions could be justified.

Practice

Are any of the following hasty generalizations?

1. The new quarterback threw two interceptions and only completed two passes in the first game. Looks like we're in for a losing season.

2. The last five times I saw Edna, she was with Vincent. They must be going out.

3. That's twice now I've had to wait for the bus because it was late. I guess buses are never on time around here.

Answers

1. Yes, this is a hasty generalization. It's only the first game, and the quarterback is new. Give him a chance to warm up!
2. Since you've seen them together five times, there's a pretty strong likelihood that Edna and Vincent are involved in some kind of relationship, so this is not a hasty generalization.
3. This is a hasty generalization. It could be you've just had bad luck the two times you wanted to ride the bus. You need to try the bus a few more times before you can comfortably conclude that the buses are always late.

▶ Biased Generalizations

On a local TV program, you hear that a recent poll shows that 85 percent of people surveyed support drilling for oil in Alaska's Arctic National Wildlife Refuge. If most Americans feel this way, you think that maybe you should rethink your position on the issue. Unfortunately, what you haven't been told is that the only people who were surveyed for this poll were employees of major oil companies.

The problem with a survey like this (there will be more on surveys in Lesson 18, "Numbers Never Lie") is that the pool of people it surveyed was *biased*. Think about it for a moment. Employees of oil companies are going to favor drilling for oil because it will generate revenue for the oil companies, which in turn means job security for the employees. Therefore, the conclusion that the majority of Americans favor drilling for oil in Alaska's Arctic National Wildlife Refuge is biased as well. It's based on a survey of biased respondents and, as a result, cannot be considered representative of Americans as a whole.

Biased generalizations can be made without using surveys as well. Any conclusion based on the testimony of someone who is biased is a **biased generalization.** For example, imagine you tell a friend that you're taking a class next fall with Professor Jenkins.

"Professor Jenkins?!" your friend replies. "She's terrible. I got an F in her class."

Should your friend's reaction change your mind about taking the class? Probably not. Your reasoning skills should tell you that your friend's conclusion about Professor Jenkins might be biased. If he got an F in her class, he isn't likely to have a very good an opinion of her.

Let's look at another example. Read the following inductive argument carefully:

All of my friends say fraternities are a waste of time. So I guess you shouldn't bother trying to join one if you don't want to waste your time.

How could this be a biased generalization? Write your answer below.

If this conclusion is based on evidence from biased sources, then the generalization (the conclusion) is biased. For example, if those friends who say that fraternities are a waste of time are also friends who had wanted to be in a fraternity but had not been invited to join, then they're likely to have a negative (biased) opinion of fraternities. Hence, their conclusion would be biased.

On the other hand, how could this be a *reliable* inductive argument? Write your answer below.

If all the friends were members of a fraternity, then this would be a much more reliable conclusion. If all the friends were members of different fraternities rather than the same one, it'd be even more reliable; their conclusion would represent a broader range of experience.

To avoid being biased, then, conclusions should be drawn only from a sample that's truly representative of the subject at hand. An inductive argument about student involvement on campus, for example, should be based on evidence from all types of students, not just those on the Student Affairs Committee.

Practice

Are any of the following biased generalizations?

4. A teacher at a meeting with ten other teachers: "The current administration doesn't care at all about educational reform, and it's the most important issue facing our nation today."
5. An employee who was laid off from his job: "That company is a terrible place to work. They laid me off!"
6. New basketball-team member who keeps getting put on the bench during games: "Everyone on the team said that Coach Adams is really tough on his team members the first season, but that if I work hard, I'll get to play in most games next season."

Answers

4. Yes, this woman's generalization—that the administration doesn't care at all about educational reform—is probably biased. Because she's a schoolteacher, she probably has different expectations for reform than most, and therefore doesn't see or appreciate the measures that the administration does take.

5. Yes, this employee's generalization is probably biased. He is making a conclusion based on only one small piece of evidence—his own misfortune at having gotten laid off. He clearly has negative feelings for the company that may not be justified.

6. Even though this player is not getting to play in the games, he has found out from all the other players on the team that the coach is hard on everyone during the first season, so his conclusion is probably fair.

► Non Sequitur

A **non sequitur** is a conclusion that does not follow logically from its premises. The problem with this fallacy is that too much of a jump is made between the premises and the conclusion. Here's an example:

Johnson is a good family man. Therefore, he will be a good politician.

It's great that Johnson is a good family man, but his devotion to his family does not necessarily mean that he'll be a good politician. Notice that this argument *assumes* that the qualities that make "a good family man" also make a good politician—and that's not necessarily, or even probably, the case. Many good family men are lousy politicians, and many good politicians are not particularly devoted to their families. The argument makes a leap—a big one—that defies logic. It's certainly possible that Johnson will be a good politician, but solely judging from the premises, it's not *likely*.

Here's another example of a *non sequitur:*

Josie is left-handed, so she'd be a good artist.

This *non sequitur* assumes that left-handed people are more artistic than right-handed people. This may sometimes be true, but it is not always the case. Furthermore, even if she is artistic, being a good artist requires inspiration and dedication, and we have no evidence that Josie has those qualities. Therefore, we can't logically conclude that Josie will be a good artist.

Here's one more:

You like cats. Cathy is a cat person, too, so you'll get along well.

What's wrong with this argument? Here, the arguer assumes that because you and Cathy are both "cat people," you will get along. But just because you both like cats doesn't mean you'll like each other. It's another *non sequitur*.

Some *non sequiturs* follow the pattern of reversing the premise and conclusion. Read the following argument, for example:

People who succeed always have clear goals. Sandra has clear goals, so she'll succeed.

Here's the argument broken down:

Premise 1: People who succeed always have clear goals.
Premise 2: Sandra has clear goals.
Conclusion: Sandra will succeed.

Though at first glance, the example may seem reasonable, in actuality, it doesn't make logical sense. That's because premise 2 and the conclusion *reverse* the claim set forth in premise 1. When parts of a claim are reversed, the argument does not stay the same. It's like saying that geniuses often have trouble in school, so someone who is having trouble in school is going to be a genius, and that's just not logical.

In Sandra's case, your critical thinking and reasoning skills should also tell you that simply because she set clear goals for herself doesn't mean they'll be achieved; hard work and dedication are also factors in the formula for success. Furthermore, the definition of *success* is something everyone determines for him- or herself.

Practice

Are there any *non sequiturs* in the following arguments?

7. Paula got straight As in her science classes. She'll make a great doctor.

8. That car is a stick shift. Most stick-shift cars get better gas mileage than automatics. You'll probably get better gas mileage if you get a stick shift.

9. Rasheed is a good accountant and he didn't even like math in school. You don't like math, so you'd make a good accountant, too.

Answers

7. Yes, this is a *non sequitur*.
8. No, this is not a *non sequitur*.
9. Yes, this is a *non sequitur*.

Practice

What assumptions do the *non sequiturs* in items 7 and 9 make?

Answers

Argument number 7 assumes that people who are good science students will also make good doctors. But being a good doctor requires more than getting good grades. It also involves years of training, an ability to handle crises, skill in dealing with patients, and much more.

In argument number 9, the second premise and conclusion reverse the first premise. Just because you don't like math doesn't mean you'll make a good accountant; what happened to Rasheed won't necessarily happen to you.

▶ In Short

When it comes to inductive arguments, you need to be on the lookout for three kinds of logical fallacies. **Hasty generalizations** draw conclusions from too little evidence. **Biased generalizations,** on the other hand, draw conclusions from *biased* evidence. Finally, *non sequiturs* jump to conclusions that defy logic; they make assumptions that don't hold water.

Skill Building until Next Time

- The next time you meet someone for the first time, be aware of how you form an opinion of him or her. Do you jump to conclusions, or do you wait until you've gathered more evidence to decide whether or not he or she would make a good friend or colleague?
- Teach a friend what you learned in this lesson. Give your friend a few of your own examples of the three fallacies.

17 ▶ Inductive Reasoning

LESSON SUMMARY

This lesson will discuss the inductive reasoning approach to determining causes. It will also go over some of the common mistakes in reasoning people make when determining cause and effect.

In Lesson 14, "Why Did it Happen?" you learned about how explanations are different from arguments. This lesson will look at a specific type of argument: the **causal argument.** The main difference between an explanation and a causal argument is simply in the way the argument is arranged. In an explanation, like in deductive reasoning, you look at the conclusion ("I was late") and then test the validity of the premises ("because my car broke down"). In a causal argument, on the other hand, the inductive approach is used: Evidence (what happened) is looked at, a conclusion is drawn about the cause based on that evidence, and then the validity of that conclusion is considered.

Just as there are criteria for testing explanations, there are also strategies for evaluating causes. Similarly, just as explanations can use false reasoning, there are also logical fallacies that can be committed in causal arguments. This chapter will start by addressing the two main strategies for determining cause and then discuss how to avoid the fallacies that often go with them.

► Determining Cause

When you are presented with an effect and want to inductively determine the cause, there are generally two techniques to use: looking for what's different and looking for what's the same.

Looking for the Difference

Your car wasn't running well on Wednesday. Normally, you use Ultra-Plus gasoline from the station down the street, but on Tuesday, you were low on gas and on cash, so you pulled into a station near your office and got half a tank of the cheapest brand. On Thursday, you went back to your regular station and filled up with your normal gas. By Friday, the car was running fine again. You did nothing else to your car, and nothing else was out of the ordinary.

So what caused the problem?

If you guessed the cheap gasoline, you're probably right. Though there are many things that can go wrong with a car and only a thorough inspection could tell for sure, the given evidence points to the cheap gas as the culprit. Why? Because the cheap gas is the **key difference**. Let's recap the facts: Your car ran well on your usual gas. When you changed the brand and grade, your car didn't run well. When you went back to your usual gas, your car ran fine again. The difference? The gasoline. Therefore, it's logical to conclude that the gasoline caused your car to run less smoothly.

Though in this example, it's obvious that the gasoline was the key difference, it isn't always so easy to determine causes. Read the following argument:

Every day for the past three months, you've been getting coffee from Lou's Deli, right around the corner from your office. One day, however, Lou's is closed, so you decide to try Moe's Deli across the street. You get your coffee and go to work. An hour later, you have a terrible stomachache. The next day, Lou's is open again and you get your usual coffee. You feel fine the rest of the day. "It must've been Moe's coffee that gave me that stomachache yesterday," you conclude.

This does seem like a logical conclusion, based on the evidence. After all, what's different between today and yesterday? It was Moe's coffee that was the difference, so Moe's coffee was the cause. Right?

Not necessarily. It is quite possible that Moe's coffee did indeed cause your stomachache. However, this conclusion can't be accepted without reservation—you can't say it's *likely* that Moe's coffee is to blame—until you ask a key question:

Were there any other relevant differences that may have caused the stomachache?

In other words, you need to consider whether there could have been something else that caused your stomachache. For example, maybe late the night before you ate spicy Chinese food. Or maybe you were really nervous about a big meeting that day. Or maybe you skipped breakfast and had an upset stomach to begin with. Any one of these possibilities could have been the cause.

The more possibilities there are, the less confident you should be that Moe's coffee is the culprit. However, if there isn't anything else unusual that you can think of, and especially if you get sick if you try Moe's again, then it's much more likely that Moe's is to blame. Either way, before you pinpoint your cause, be sure to consider whether or not there could be other relevant differences.

Practice

Answer the following questions carefully.

1. Is the following a logical causal argument? Why or why not?

Halcyon Café used to be packed every Sunday night when A.B. Gomez was there to DJ. Since they hired a new DJ to replace A.B. Gomez, though, Halcyon empties out by Sunday afternoon after brunch—only a small crowd now shows up on Sunday nights. It must be that people don't like the new DJ.

2. You have a small dog, and you decide to take her to the new dog run in your neighborhood on Monday morning. On Monday evening, your friend, who has just gotten a new puppy, asks if she can bring the puppy to your house to play with your dog. On Tuesday morning, you notice that you have several flea bites on your ankles. You conclude

   a. your dog picked up fleas at the dog run.
   b. your dog picked up fleas from your friend's puppy.
   c. either **a** or **b**.
   d. **a** and **b**.

Answers

   1. Yes, this is a logical casual argument. Whether it's because there is a new DJ that doesn't have as big a fan base as the previous one, or whether it's simply because the people don't like the music that the new DJ is playing, changing the DJ is very likely to have caused the decrease in attendance on Sunday nights. You should consider, though, whether or not there have been other relevant changes in the café, like new hours, new management, or new prices.

   2. While all of these choices are possibilities, the best choice is **d**. Your dog could just as easily have picked up fleas from other dogs at the dog run as she could have from your friend's new puppy. Furthermore, since your dog is exposed to both situations on the same day, she could have picked up fleas both times.

Looking for the Common Denominator

Sometimes, the cause can be determined not by looking for what's different, but by looking for what's the *same*—that is, something that each incident has in common. Take the following scenario, for example:

Jason has been having trouble sleeping a few nights a week. On the nights when he can't sleep, he notices that the neighbor's dog is always barking and howling. Jason concludes that his trouble sleeping is due to the dog.

Jason has used a logical approach to determine the cause of his insomnia. He's looking for a pattern—something that is consistent with the nights he can't sleep. Because he hears the dog barking and howling on all of those nights, it could be that the dog is preventing him from getting his sleep. The dog is the **common denominator** for all of these occasions.

Just as it is important to be careful not to overlook other possible differences, however, it's important to remember to look for other possible common denominators. Before Jason concludes that his sleeplessness is because of the dog barking, he should carefully consider whether there might be anything else in common on those nights that he can't sleep.

So let's complicate the situation just a bit by adding more evidence from which to draw your conclusion.

Jason has been having trouble sleeping a few nights a week. On the nights when he can't sleep, he notices that the neighbor's dog is always barking. He also realizes that the sleepless nights are always nights that he hasn't talked to his girlfriend. Those are also nights that he skipped going to the gym because he worked late. What's causing Jason to have trouble sleeping?

   a. the dog barking
   b. not talking to his girlfriend
   c. not exercising
   d. none of the above

Can you answer this question with confidence? Probably not. That's because each of these answers is a legitimate possibility. Each situation occurs on the nights Jason can't sleep. Just like the coffee wasn't the only thing different in the previous scenario, here, the dog isn't the only common denominator. There are many possibilities. If you're to confidently say which of these is the cause, you need to pinpoint just one event in common with all the bad nights.

If Jason knew that the dog barked *every* night—even on those nights when he is able to sleep—then the barking dog could be eliminated as an option. Similarly, if Jason skips the gym on other occasions when he *can* sleep, then choice **c** could be eliminated. But until more evidence is given and the other possibilities can be eliminated, none of the choices can be chosen over the others.

Practice

Read the following scenario and then answer the questions that follow.

It's summer and Barbara has been eating less than usual. She notices that on the especially hot days, her appetite is low.

3. Can Barbara say with confidence that the heat is causing her to lose her appetite?

4. What other possible common denominators could there be for Barbara's condition?

Answers

3. Barbara can say this with confidence only if she has carefully checked for other possible common denominators. If nothing else happens on the days when she has a loss of appetite, then Barbara can safely conclude that it's the heat.

4. Barbara's loss of appetite may have to do with worries about work, relationships, money, etc.; pressure or stress; illness; a change in diet; and/or a combination of these and other possible factors.

▶ Post Hoc, Ergo Propter Hoc

Nina, who'd always dressed rather plainly, decided it was time to jazz up her wardrobe. She went shopping and bought a closet full of new, brightly colored clothing. Two weeks later, she was promoted at work. "Wow," she told her friend, "I had no idea that what I wore to work could make such a difference. Just changing my wardrobe finally got me that promotion I'd been waiting for!"

Nina deserves congratulations, but not for her reasoning. What's wrong with her logic here?

Nina has committed the ***post hoc, ergo propter hoc*** inductive reasoning fallacy. *Post hoc, ergo propter hoc* literally means *after this, therefore because of this.* Nina has assumed that because her promotion came *after* she changed her wardrobe, her promotion was *caused* by her change in wardrobe. Maybe, just maybe, her appearance did have something to do with it. But in all likelihood, there were several other causes for her promotion. She'd probably been doing good work for months or years, for one thing, and the position to which she had been promoted may not have been vacant before. There may be several other reasons as well.

Of course, cause and effect *is* a chronological structure—the cause must come before the effect—but remember that you need to consider other possible causes. Just because *A* comes before *B* doesn't mean there's a logical connection between the two events.

Here's another example of *post hoc*:

After the Citizens First Bill was passed, crime in this area skyrocketed. Funny how the bill that was supposed to *reduce* crime actually *increased* it!

Notice how this argument assumes that because the Citizens First Bill came first and the rise in crime came second, one *caused* the other. But proving that there's a link between the two events would not be easy, especially since an increased crime rate could be caused by many different factors. In fact, a figure as complicated as crime rate is probably caused by a *multitude* of factors. What else can you think of that might have caused the increase in crime?

Other possible causes:

You may have listed other possible causes like the following:

- An increase in unemployment
- A recession
- A change in population in the area
- A reduction in the police force

In fact, because human society is so complex, most social issues have multiple causes. In all likelihood, the increase in crime was caused by a combination of these, and possibly other, factors. But the Citizens First Bill, unless it specifically cut jobs and reduced the police force, is not to blame. It may have come first, but it's not necessarily the cause.

Practice

Do any of the following causal arguments commit the *post hoc* fallacy?

5. I used to drink four or five cups of coffee a day and I had lots of headaches. Now that I quit drinking coffee, my headaches are gone.

6. After we got our new vacuum cleaner, our electric bills skyrocketed. That thing might as well suck the money right out of our pockets!

7. Mandy started feeding her two-year-old an extra-fortified oatmeal for breakfast, and as a result, he's grown two inches in the last two months!

Answers

5. This seems like a reasonable argument, not a *post hoc* error. Part of what makes this logical is the general knowledge that caffeine can cause headaches in some drinkers as its effect wears off.

6. *Post hoc.* Chances are that unless you vacuum every room every day and you have a big house, the vacuum cleaner won't have much effect on your electric bill. More likely, your utility company has raised your rates and/or you're simply using your other appliances more.

7. *Post hoc.* Babies grow in fits and spurts. Maybe the oatmeal is helping, but there are too many other possible causes for this person to assume the growth is due to the fortified cereal.

► The Chicken or the Egg?

"I'll tell you why people today have short attention spans," your friend says to you one day. "It's because we are living in such a fast-paced society."

Maybe—but this is not necessarily true. Before you accept your friend's theory, consider that he could have just as easily argued the reverse:

"We are living in a fast-paced society because people have such short attention spans today."

Which argument is the right one? Does living in a fast-paced society cause short attention spans, or do we live in a fast-paced society because people have short attention spans?

Again, both arguments try to simplify a topic that's very complicated. It's very hard to know what came first, a fast-paced society or short attention spans—the **chicken or egg dilemma**. You need to think carefully about the relationship between the two events before you come to any conclusions.

Here's another example:

Lucy feels more confident because she aced her last two exams.

True, getting good grades can boost your self-esteem. But it is also true that someone who feels confident is likely to perform better on an exam than someone who does not. So this is another case where cause and effect could go either way: Lucy's increased confidence could be caused by her good grades, but it's equally likely that her good grades were caused by her increased confidence. In such a case, it's best to suspend judgment about the cause until more information is known.

Practice

Read the following carefully. Are any guilty of taking sides in the chicken or egg dilemma?

8. People don't have family values anymore. That's because so many people get divorced these days.

9. Since Linda started exercising, she feels a lot better about herself.

10. There are so many computer manufacturers because the cost of computer technology is so low.

Answers

8. Guilty. It's just as easy to argue that "so many people get divorced these days because people don't have family values anymore." As with any social issue, there are certain to be multiple causes.

9. Though it *is* possible to argue the reverse, it's pretty likely that Linda's exercise is indeed responsible for her increased self-esteem.

10. Guilty. This is another chicken or egg dilemma. The low cost of technology could just as likely be the result of so many different companies working to develop more cost-effective products and procedures. This case needs further investigation.

▶ In Short

There are two main approaches to determining causes in inductive reasoning: looking for what's different and looking for the common denominator. It is important to remember to look for other possible differences or common causes. Causal arguments should avoid the ***post hoc, ergo propter hoc*** fallacy, which assumes that because *A* came before *B*, *A caused B*. Finally, some causal arguments fall into the **chicken or egg** trap, where the argument that *A* caused *B* is just as strong as the argument that *B* caused *A*. Think carefully before accepting such an argument.

Skill Building until Next Time

- Be on the lookout this week for errors in causal reasoning. People are often quick to assign cause and neglect to think about other possible differences or common denominators. See if you can catch others—or even yourself—making these mistakes and correct them.
- Read some history. Historical texts explore cause and effect in detail, and they'll help you see just how complicated causes can sometimes be. This will help you realize how careful you need to be when evaluating cause and effect.

18▶ Numbers Never Lie

LESSON SUMMARY

Statistics are often used to strengthen arguments—but they aren't always trustworthy. This lesson will show you how to judge the validity of statistics and how to make sure that any statistics you cite are credible.

There's strength in numbers. Whether on the battlefield or in the boardroom, the more people you have fighting for a cause, the more likely you are to win. There's strength in numbers in arguments, too—statistics generally carry more weight and sound more valid than opinions. That's because numbers look concrete, factual, and objective. But numbers are not always to be trusted. Like words, numbers can be—and often are—manipulated. As a critical thinker, you need to beware of the kinds of tricks numbers can play, and you need to know how to evaluate surveys, statistics, and other figures before you accept them as valid.

▶ First Things First: Consider the Source

One of your first priorities when you come across a figure or statistic is to consider the source. Where is this information coming from? You need to know the source so you can consider its credibility.

Figures are often cited without naming their source. This should automatically raise a red flag. When there's no source acknowledged, that figure could come from anywhere. Here's an example:

Eighty percent of all Americans believe that there is too much violence on television.

Our immediate reaction might be to say "Wow! Eighty percent! That's an impressive statistic." But because this claim does not indicate a source, you have to fight your instinct to accept the number as true. The question, "Who conducted this survey?" must be answered in order for you to be able to assess the validity of the figure. A figure that isn't backed by a credible source isn't worth much and can't be accepted with confidence. Unfortunately, you have to consider that the claimant could have made it up to give the *appearance* of statistical support for his argument.

If the claimant does provide a source, then the next step is to consider the credibility of that source. Remember, to determine credibility, look for evidence of bias and level of expertise.

Here's that statistic again attributed to two different sources:

1. According to Parents Against Television Violence, 80 percent of Americans believe that there is too much violence on TV.
2. According to a recent University of Minnesota survey, 80 percent of Americans believe there is too much violence on TV.

Would you accept the statistic as offered by source number 1? How about by source number 2?

While both sources may have a respectable level of expertise, it should be acknowledged that the people who conducted the university study probably have a higher level of expertise. More importantly, the source in number 1—Parents Against Television Violence—should encourage you to consider their statistics with caution. Is a group such as PATV likely to be biased in the issue of television violence? Absolutely. Is it possible, then, that such an organization could offer false or misleading statistics to support its cause? Yes. Would it be wise, therefore, to accept this statistic only with some reservations? Yes.

The university's study, however, is much more likely to have been conducted professionally and accurately. Scholarly research is subject to rigorous scrutiny by the academic community, so the university's findings are probably quite accurate and acceptable. There's less reason to suspect bias or sloppy statistical methods.

Practice

Evaluate the following statistics. Are the sources credible? Why or why not?

1. A survey conducted by the California Lettuce Growers Association shows that four out of five people disapprove of the Farm Redistribution Act.

2. According to the Federal Drug Administration, 67 percent of Americans worry about toxic chemicals on their fruits and vegetables.

Answers

1. This source has a respectable level of expertise, but you should consider its potential for bias. Given the source, there is a possibility that the survey was skewed to show such a high disapproval rating.
2. Because the FDA is a government organization whose credibility rests on its awareness of food and drug dangers to American citizens, this statistic can probably be trusted.

► The Importance of Sample Size

In the ideal survey or opinion poll, *everyone* in the population in question would be surveyed. But since this is often impossible, researchers have to make do by interviewing a **sample** of the population. Unfortunately, this means that their results do not always reflect the sentiment of the entire population.

Obviously, the larger the sample size, the more reflective the survey will be of the entire population. For example, let's say you want to know how parents of children in grades 6–9 in Pennsylvania public schools feel about removing vending machines from school cafeterias. If there are two million parents that fall into this category, how many should you survey? Two? Two hundred? Two thousand? Twenty thousand? Two hundred thousand?

Indeed, how many people you survey depends upon the time and money you have to invest in the survey. But under no circumstances would surveying two or two hundred people be sufficient—these numbers represent far too small a percentage of the population that you're surveying. Twenty thousand is a much better sample, although it constitutes only one percent of the population you are trying to reach. Two hundred thousand, on the other hand, reaches ten percent of the population, making it much more likely that the results of your survey accurately reflect the population as a whole.

On NBC TV's news magazine *Dateline*, commentator Storm Phillips often ends the show with the results of a *Dateline* opinion poll. Before announcing the results, however, *Dateline* tells its viewers exactly how many people were surveyed. That is, *Dateline* lets you know the exact sample size. This practice helps make the reported results more credible and enables you to judge for yourself whether a sample is large enough to be representative of the sentiments of the entire country.

You're probably wondering how much is enough when it comes to sample size. There's no hard and fast rule here except one: The larger your sample size, the better. The bigger the sample, the more likely it is that your survey results will accurately reflect the opinions of the population in question.

Practice

3. Read the following situation carefully and answer the question that follows.

   You're conducting a survey of college students to determine how many support the administration's proposal to raise tuition so that there will be enough funds to build a new sports arena. There are 5,000 students. You've set up a small polling booth in the student union. After how many responses would you feel you have a sample large enough to reflect the opinion of the entire student body?

   a. 5
   b. 50
   c. 500
   d. 1,000

Answer

Five hundred responses (**c**) would probably be sufficient to give you a good idea of the overall sentiment on campus. If you could get 1,000 responses, however, your results would be much more accurate. Both 5 and 50 are far too small for sample sizes in this survey.

► Representative, Random, and Biased Samples

Let's say you want to conduct the "tuition/sports arena" survey but don't have any budget. Since you are on a tennis team with 50 players, you decide to simply poll the players on your team. Will your results accurately reflect the sentiment on your campus?

Regardless of how the players feel about this issue, it'd be nearly impossible for your survey results to accurately reflect the sentiments of the student body. Why? Because your sample is not **representative** of the population whose opinion you wish to reflect. In order for your sample to be representative, it should include *all* the various groups and subgroups within the student population. That is, the people in your sample group should represent the people in the whole group. That means, for one thing, that you need to survey players from several different sports teams, not just yours. In addition, your sample group needs to include members from *all* different campus organizations—student government, sororities, political groups, various clubs, and so on.

Furthermore, the sample should include respondents from these groups in approximately the same proportion that you would find them on campus. That is, if 50 percent of the students belong to fraternities or sororities, then approximately 50 percent of your respondents should be members of fraternities or sororities. If 20 percent are members of an athletic group, then approximately 20 percent of your respondents should be athletes, and so on. In this way, your survey results are more likely to be proportionate to the results you'd get if you were able to survey everyone on campus.

But how do you get a representative sample for larger populations such as two million parents or one billion Chinese? Because the range of respondents is so wide, your best bet is to get a **random** sample. By randomly selecting participants, you have the best chance of getting a representative sample because each person in the population has the same chance of being surveyed. Representative and random samples help prevent you from having a **biased** sample. Imagine you read the following:

> In a survey of 6,000 city residents, 79 percent of the respondents say that the Republican mayor has done an outstanding job.

This claim tells us the sample size—6,000—which is a substantive number. But it doesn't tell how the 6,000 residents were chosen to answer the survey. Because the political affiliation and socioeconomic standing of the respondents could greatly influence the results of the survey, it is important to know if those 6,000 people are varied enough to accurately reflect the sentiment of an entire city.

For example, if all of those 6,000 surveyed were Republicans, of course the percentage of favorable votes would be high; but that doesn't tell much about how people from other political parties feel. Survey another 6,000 residents who are Democrats and you'd come up with a much, much lower number. Why? Because members of this sample group, due to their socioeconomic status and/or their political beliefs, might be biased *against* a Republican mayor. Thus, it's critical that the sample be as representative as possible, including both Democrats and Republicans, the wealthy and the poor.

How do you know, though, that a survey has used a representative sample? Surveys that have been conducted legitimately will generally be careful to provide you with information about the sample size and population so that their results are more credible to you. You might see something like the following, for example:

- In a recent survey, 500 random shoppers were asked whether they felt the Food Court in the mall provides a sufficient selection.
- A survey of 3,000 men between the ages of 18 and 21 found that 72 percent think either that the drinking age should be lowered to 18 or that the draft age should be raised to 21.

Notice how these claims let you know exactly who was surveyed.

Special Note

Beware of call-in surveys and polls that are conducted by mail or that otherwise depend upon the *respondents* to take action. Results of these surveys tend to be misleading because those who take the time to return mail-in surveys or make the effort to call, fax, or e-mail a response are often people who feel very strongly about the issue. To assume that the opinions of those people who feel strongly about the issue represents how the entire population feels is risky because it's not very likely that *most* people in the population feel that way.

Practice

Evaluate the following claims. Do the surveys seem to have representative samples, or could the samples be biased?

4. **Topic:** Should campus security be tighter?
   Population: Female students
   Sample: Women who have been victims of crimes on campus

5. **Topic:** Is there sufficient parking in the city?
   Population: City residents and visitors
   Sample: People randomly stopped on the street in various districts within the city

6. **Topic:** Should Braxton Elementary extend school hours until 4:00 P.M?
   Population: All parents of children in Braxton Elementary
   Sample: Members of the PTA

Answers

4. The sample in this survey is clearly biased. If only women who have been victims of crime on campus are surveyed, the results will certainly reflect a dissatisfaction with campus security. Furthermore, unless this is an all-female college, the sample is not representative.

5. The sample in this survey is representative. People randomly stopped on the street in various parts of the city should result in a good mix of residents and visitors with all kinds of backgrounds and parking needs.

6. This sample is not representative. Only a limited number of parents are able to find the time—or have the desire—to join the PTA. Parents who hold down two jobs, for example, aren't likely to be members, but their opinion about the extended school day is very important.

▶ Comparing Apples and Oranges

In 1972, a Hershey's chocolate bar cost only 5 cents. Today, the same bar costs at least 50 cents. That's an increase of over 1,000 percent!

This increase sounds extreme, doesn't it? But is it really as severe as the math makes it seem? Not quite.

The problem with this claim is that while the actual price of a Hershey's bar may have increased 1,000 percent, it's not a fair comparison. That's because 5 cents in 1972 had more market value than 5 cents today. In this situation, the actual costs can't legitimately be compared. Instead, the costs have to be compared after they've been *adjusted for inflation*. Because there has been such a long time span and the value of the dollar has declined in the last 30 years, maybe 50 cents today is actually cheaper than 5 cents was in 1972.

It's important, therefore, to analyze comparisons like this to be sure the statistics are indeed comparable. Any monetary comparison needs to take into consideration market value and inflation. When dealing with figures other than money, however, there are other important concerns. For example, read the following argument:

In 1990, there were 100 unemployed people in Boone County. In 2000, there were 250. That's an increase of 150 percent in just ten years. Unemployment in this country is becoming an epidemic!

What's wrong with this argument? Clearly, there has been a sharp rise in unemployment in the last decade. But what the claim doesn't tell you is that during that same time period, the population of Boone County increased by 250 percent. Now how does that affect the argument?

If the population increased from 100,000 to 350,000, is the rise in unemployment still evidence that can be used to support the claim "Unemployment in this country is becoming an epidemic"? No. In fact, this means that that the number of unemployed per capita (that is, per person) has actually decreased. This is a case of comparing apples to oranges because the population in 1990 was so different than the population in 2000.

You should beware of any comparison across time, but the same problems can arise in contemporary comparisons. Take the following statistic, for example:

Charleston Medical Center physicians perform more arthroscopic knee operations than St. Francis physicians, who use a technique that requires a large incision.

If you need to have knee surgery, should you go to Charleston Medical Center? Not necessarily. Consider this fact, first: St. Francis physicians specialize in complicated knee surgeries that cannot be performed arthroscopically. Because their pool of patients is different from those of Charleston Medical Center, so will the number of nonarthroscopic knee operations.

Practice

Do the following statistics compare apples and oranges, or are they fair comparisons?

7. I bought this house in 1964 for just $28,000. Now it's worth $130,000. What a profit I've made!

8. That shirt is $45. This one is only $15. They look exactly the same. I found a bargain!

9. The total per capita income in Jewel County, adjusted for inflation, went up 12 percent in the last two years.

Answers

7. Apples and oranges. When this figure is adjusted for inflation, you might see that the house has the same market value.

8. This depends upon what the shirts are made of. If they're both made of the same type and quality of material, then it's an apples to apples comparison. If, however, one shirt is made of silk and the other polyester, then it's apples and oranges.

9. Fair.

▶ In Short

The truth about statistics is that they can be very misleading. When you come across statistics, check the source to see whether or not it's credible. Then find out the sample size and decide whether it's substantial enough. Look for evidence that the sample is representative of the population whose opinion you wish to reflect, or randomly selected and not biased. Finally, beware of statistics that compare apples to oranges by putting two unequal items side by side.

Skill Building until Next Time

- Look for survey results in a reputable newspaper with a national circulation, like *The New York Times, Washington Post,* or *San Francisco Chronicle.* Notice how much information they provide about how the survey was conducted. Then, look for survey results in a tabloid or a less credible source. Notice how little information is provided and check for the possibility of bias.
- Think about a survey that you would like to conduct. Who is your target population? How would you ensure a representative sample? How large should your sample be?

19 ▶ Problem Solving Revisited

LESSON SUMMARY

Logic problems and puzzles can be fun, but they can also help determine the direction of your career if you ever have to take an exam that tests your logic and reasoning skills. This lesson will show you what types of questions you'll typically find on such an exam and how to tackle those kinds of questions.

Strong critical thinking and reasoning skills will help you make better decisions and solve problems more effectively on a day-to-day basis. But they'll also help you in special situations, such as when you are being tested on your logic and reasoning skills. For example, you may be taking a critical thinking class, applying for a promotion, or hoping to be a police officer or fireman—or maybe you just like to solve logic problems and puzzles for fun. Whatever the case, if you find yourself facing logic problems, you'll see they generally come in the form of questions that test your:

- Common sense
- Ability to distinguish good evidence from bad evidence
- Ability to draw logical conclusions from evidence

You've been learning a lot about critical thinking and deductive and inductive reasoning, so you should already have the skills to tackle these kinds of questions. This lesson aims to familiarize you with the format of these kinds of test questions and to provide you with strategies for getting to the correct answer quickly.

▶ Common Sense

Questions that test your common sense often present you with decision-making scenarios. Though the situation may be foreign to you and the questions may seem complicated, you can find the answer by remembering how to break a problem down into its parts and by thinking logically about the situation.

Sample Question

Read the following question:

A police officer arrives at the scene of a two-car accident. In what order should the officer do the following?

I. Interview witnesses.
II. Determine if anyone needs immediate medical attention.
III. Move the vehicles off of the roadway.
IV. Interview the drivers to find out what happened.

a. II, IV, III, I
b. II, IV, I, III
c. II, III, I, IV
d. IV, II, III, I

The best answer is **b**, II, IV, I, III. Your common sense should tell you that no matter what, the first priority is the safety of the people involved in the crash. That's why **II** has to come first on the list—and that means you can automatically eliminate answer **d**. Now, again using your common sense, what should come next? While statements from witnesses are important, it's more important to speak directly to the people involved in the accident, so **IV** should follow **II**—and that eliminates answer **c**. Now you're down to **a** and **b**. Now why should you wait to move the vehicles out of the roadway? The main reason this doesn't come earlier is because you need to see the evidence—exactly where and how the cars ended up—as you listen to driver and witness testimony. Once you have their statements and have recorded the scene, *then* you can safely move the vehicles.

Practice

1. Using the previous scenario and, assuming that both drivers are in critical condition, write three things that the officer should do and the order in which he or she should do them.

   1.

   2.

   3.

Answer

Again, common sense should tell you that the first thing you need to do is get the drivers medical attention. Number one on your list, then, should be *call an ambulance*. What next? Depending upon the type of accident, the drivers may be in danger if they remain in the cars. Therefore, the next thing the officer should do is *quickly assess the damage to the cars* so that he or she can move the passengers to safety if there's a danger of an explosion. Finally, the police officer may not be a medic, but chances are, he or she has some basic medical training. The next thing the police officer should do is *check to see if there's emergency care he or she can administer*. Perhaps the officer can administer CPR or bandage a badly bleeding wound until the ambulance arrives.

Remember, the key to answering this type of question is to remember how to prioritize issues, and that means you need to think carefully about many different possible scenarios.

Practice

2. Jonathan wants to run for president of the senior class. In what order should he do the following?

    I. Come up with a catchy campaign slogan.
    II. Develop a campaign platform.
    III. Find out the procedures and requirements for running for class office.
    IV. Create posters and post them all around the school.

    a. I, II, III, IV
    b. II, I, IV, III
    c. III, II, I, IV
    d. III, I, II, IV

Answer

The best answer is **c.** Without question, the first thing Jonathan needs to do is find out the proper procedures and requirements for running for class office. Maybe in order to run for president, Jonathan must have a grade point average of 3.0. If Jonathan doesn't have that average and hasn't bothered to check the requirements before doing **I, II,** and **IV,** he's wasting his time and energy. Logic should also tell you that Jonathan has to develop a campaign platform before he should come up with a slogan and posters. After all, shouldn't his slogan and posters reflect what he plans to do as senior class president? Finally, Jonathan should want to have his slogan—a catchy phrase that can easily be remembered—on all of his posters, so the posters are clearly the last of Jonathan's steps.

▶ Evaluating Evidence

Logic tests often measure deductive as well as inductive reasoning skills. That's why some questions may ask you to evaluate evidence. Remember, strong evidence for a deductive argument is both *credible* and *reasonable*.

Sample Question

You'll need to keep these criteria in mind and use your common sense to work your way through problems like the following:

Karen has complained to her supervisor that the company provides the math department with more technological amenities than it does the English department. Which of the following would provide the strongest support for her claim?

a. All the people in the English department agree with Karen.

b. The 30 people in the English department have only one printer and one fax machine, whereas the 35 people in the math department have three printers, three fax machines, and a scanner.

c. There are 8 percent more people in the math department than in the English department.

d. The English department prints more documents than the math department does.

You should have selected **b** as the answer. Why? Because **b** provides the most specific and relevant support for the argument. Though there is strength in numbers and it helps that all the people in the English department support Karen's claim (choice **a**), Karen is more likely to convince the management by citing concrete statistics. It's clear from the numbers provided in choice **b** that the math department does indeed have more technological amenities than the English department does. Choice **c** isn't the strongest piece of evidence because it merely states that there is a small percentage difference between the amount of employees in the math and English departments, without relating this fact to the issue at hand—the technological amenities. Choice **d**, while it could be used to support Karen's claim, is not as strong as **b**, because it also doesn't directly address the amenities.

Now it's your turn.

Practice

Read the following scenario carefully and answer the questions that follow.

City Council member Andrew Anderson claims that the city could save millions of dollars each year by turning services like garbage collection over to private companies.

3. Which of the following would provide the strongest support for Anderson's argument?
   a. statistics showing how much the city spends each year on these services
   b. statistics showing how much comparable cities have saved by farming out these services to private companies
   c. proposals from private companies showing how well they could perform these services for the city and at what costs
   d. a direct comparison of how much the city spends per year on these services and how much the city would save by farming the services out to private companies

4. Which of the following is most likely to work against Anderson's argument?
   a. statements from citizens protesting the switch from public to private services
   b. statistics demonstrating how much more the average citizen would have to pay for privatization of these services
   c. reports from other cities with privatized services about citizen protests that forced the return to public services
   d. reports from other cities about corruption among privatized service providers

Answers

3. The strongest support for Anderson's argument is **d,** a direct comparison of how much the city spends per year on these services and how much the city would save by farming the services out to private companies. Remember, Anderson's argument is that the city could save millions by turning these services over to the private sector, and this comparison would show exactly how much this city (not other cities) would save.

4. Answer **c** is most likely to work against Anderson's argument because it is the strongest evidence that the plan didn't work in similar cities. Furthermore, it shows that city councils that had approved similar plans had to reinstate public services due to citizen protests. Since city council members are elected officials, it's important for them to keep their constituents happy, and **c** suggests privatizing these services does not keep citizens happy. Furthermore, you should be able to see that **a, b,** and **d** are all reasons that would be likely to cause citizens to protest and demand a return to public services.

▶ Drawing Conclusions from Evidence

Many questions you face when you're being tested on your reasoning skills will ask you to draw conclusions from evidence. You've completed several lessons on inductive reasoning, so you should be quite good at these questions, even if their format is different from what you're used to.

As in the other types of questions, you can help ensure a correct response by using the process of elimination. Given the evidence the question provides, you should automatically be able to eliminate some of the answers.

Sample Question

For example, read the following question:

A jeep has driven off the road and hit a tree. There are skid marks along the road for several yards leading up to a dead fawn. The marks then swerve to the right and off the road, stopping where the jeep is. The impact with the tree is head-on, but the damage is not severe. Based on the evidence, which of the following is most likely what happened?

a. The driver was aiming for the fawn and lost control of the jeep.

b. The driver fell asleep at the wheel and was awakened when he hit the fawn.

c. The driver tried to avoid the fawn and lost control of the jeep.

d. The driver was drunk and out of control.

Given the facts—especially the key fact that there are skid marks—you can automatically eliminate choices **a** and **b.** If the driver were aiming for the fawn, he probably wouldn't have hit the brakes and created skid marks. Instead, he probably would have accelerated, in which case, his impact with the tree would have been harder and resulted in more damage. Similarly, if the driver had fallen asleep at the wheel and only woken up when he hit the fawn, there wouldn't have been skid marks leading up to the fawn.

So now you're down to two possibilities: **c** and **d.** Which is more likely to be true? While it is entirely possible that the driver was drunk, all of the evidence points to **c** as the most likely possibility. The skid marks indicate that the driver was trying to stop to avoid hitting the fawn. Unsuccessful, he hit the animal and swerved off the road into a tree.

Other questions that ask you to draw conclusions from evidence may vary in format, but don't let their appearance throw you. If you read the following practice problems, for example, you'll see that you can tackle them quickly and easily by applying the evidence that's provided and eliminating the incorrect answers as you go along.

Practice

5. There are four brothers—Al, Bob, Carl, and Dave. Dave is two years older than Bob; Bob is one year younger than Carl; Al, who is 34, is two years younger than Carl. Which brother is oldest?

a. Al

b. Bob

c. Carl

d. Dave

6. Jack and Allison are planning the seating arrangements for their wedding reception. At one table are six guests. When deciding who should sit next to whom at this table, the couple has to keep in mind that:

- Guest 1 cannot sit next to Guest 2.
- Guests 3 and 4 must sit next to each other, but under no circumstances should Guest 4 sit next to Guest 1.
- Guest 5 can sit next to anyone except Guest 3.
- Guest 6 should not sit next to Guest 3 or 4 and would be happiest sitting next to Guest 5.

Which of the following is the best arrangement for this table?

a. **b.** **c.**

Answers

5. You can solve this puzzle easily by starting with this key fact: Al is 34 years old. Because you know Al's age, you can then determine that Carl is 36. That eliminates Al as the oldest. Then from Carl's age, you can determine that Bob is 35; that eliminates Bob, too. From Bob's age, you can determine that Dave is 37. That makes Dave the oldest and **d** the correct answer.

6. Though the question seems complicated, the answer is really quite simply achieved. Start with this key piece of information—3 and 4 must sit next to each other and 4 cannot sit with 1. Why is this the key piece? Because it allows you to seat three of the six guests immediately. Then the other three should easily fall into place and you can see that choice **a** is the correct answer.

▶ In Short

Tests that aim to measure your critical thinking and reasoning skills generally ask three types of questions: those that measure your common sense, those that measure your ability to recognize good evidence, and those that measure your ability to draw logical conclusions from evidence. You'll perform well on these tests if you remember to break down the parts of a problem and think about different possible scenarios, keep in mind the criteria for strong arguments and good evidence, and start inductive reasoning questions by working with the key facts. Use the process of elimination to help you arrive at the correct answer.

Skill Building until Next Time

- Stop in your local bookstore or go to the library and get a book of logic problems and puzzles. The more you practice them, the better you'll get at solving them.
- Write your own logic problems and puzzles. Test them out on your family and friends. Be sure you can clearly explain the correct answer.

20 ▶ Putting It All Together

LESSON SUMMARY

This lesson puts together the strategies and skills you've learned throughout this book, particularly in Lessons 11–19. You'll review the key points of these lessons and practice both your inductive and deductive reasoning skills.

Before you begin "putting it all together," let's review what you've learned in the second half of this book. If you'd like a quick review of the first half, turn to Lesson 10.

▶ Lesson 11: Logical Fallacies: Appeals to Emotion

You learned that people will often try to convince you to accept their claims by appealing to your emotions rather than to your sense of reason. They may use *scare tactics*, *flattery*, or *peer pressure*, or they may appeal to your *sense of pity*.

▶ Lesson 12: Logical Fallacies: The Impostors

You learned about four logical fallacies that pretend to be logical but don't hold water. *No in-betweens* claims that there are only two choices when, in fact, there are many. The *slippery slope* fallacy argues that if X happens, then

Y will follow, even though *X* doesn't necessarily lead to *Y*. *Circular reasoning* is an argument that goes in a circle—the premises simply restate the conclusion. And *two wrongs make a right* argues that it's okay to do something to someone else because someone else might do that same thing to you.

Lesson 13: Logical Fallacies: Distracters and Distorters

You learned how to recognize three common logical fallacies that divert your attention and distort the issue. An *ad hominem* fallacy attacks the *person* instead of attacking the claims that that person makes. A *red herring* distracts you by bringing in an irrelevant issue, while the *straw man* distorts the opponent's position so that the opponent is easier to knock down.

Lesson 14: Why Did It Happen?

You practiced evaluating explanations for validity. You learned that explanations must be relevant and testable and that you should reject explanations that are circular. You also learned the importance of being wary of explanations that contradict your existing knowledge or accepted theories.

Lesson 15: Inductive Reasoning

You learned that inductive reasoning is the process of drawing logical conclusions from evidence. You also learned that a good inductive argument is one in which it is very *likely* that the premises lead to the conclusion.

Lesson 16: Jumping to Conclusions

You learned to distinguish between good inductive reasoning and inductive fallacies like *hasty generalizations*, which draw conclusions from too little evidence. *Biased generalizations* draw conclusions from biased evidence, and *non sequiturs* draw conclusions that don't logically follow from the premises.

Lesson 17: Inductive Reasoning

You learned the two inductive reasoning approaches to determining cause: looking for what's different and looking for the common denominator. You learned to look for other possible differences and common causes and to watch out for the *post hoc, ergo propter hoc* fallacy—assuming that because *A* came before *B*, *A* caused *B*. You also learned how to avoid the "chicken or egg" causal argument.

Lesson 18: Numbers Never Lie

You learned that numbers can be very misleading. You practiced checking statistics for a *reliable source*, an adequate *sample size*, and a *representative sample*. You also learned how to recognize statistics that compare "apples and oranges."

Lesson 19: Problem Solving Revisited

You put your critical thinking and deductive and inductive reasoning skills to work on the kind of questions you might find on a logic or reasoning skills exam. You solved logic problems designed to test your common sense, ability to recognize good evidence, and ability to draw logical conclusions from evidence.

> **If any of these terms or strategies sound unfamiliar to you, STOP. Take a few minutes to review whatever lessons remain unclear.**

Practice

Now it's time to pull all of these ideas together, add them to what you learned in the first half of the book, and tackle the following practice exercises.

Read the following passage carefully and then answer the questions that follow.

Stop tropical deforestation! Now is the time to put a permanent stop to tropical deforestation. If we don't act now, there soon will be thousands of companies destroying our world's most bountiful gardens and, in the process, unleashing carbon dioxide into the atmosphere. Do you want future generations to be exposed to this deadly gas that causes a massive, gaping hole in the ozone and contributes to disastrous global warming? Do you want to be part of a generation that is responsible for destroying the habitat (murdering a culture!) of indigenous tribes of people that live in rainforests? Research shows that 75 percent of Americans are against tropical deforestation!

1. Which deductive reasoning fallacy is used in this passage?
   a. circular reasoning
   b. euphemisms
   c. slippery slope
   d. straw man

2. The term "deadly gas" is a(n)
   a. euphemism.
   b. dysphemism.
   c. *ad hominem.*
   d. hasty generalization.

3. The question, "Do you want to be part of a generation that is responsible for destroying the habitat (murdering a culture!) of indigenous tribes of people that live in rainforests?" is a(n)
   a. euphemism.
   b. appeal to pity.
   c. *non sequitur.*
   d. biased question.

4. Why is the claim, "Research shows that 75 percent of Americans are against tropical deforestation!" flawed?
   a. It doesn't tell who the researchers are (who conducted the study).
   b. It doesn't give the sample size.
   c. It doesn't tell who was surveyed.
   d. all of the above

5. Does the argument provide any credible facts? If so, write them below. If not, are there any claims that can be accepted as tentative truths?

The following items (6–10) present questions, statements, or short passages that illustrate the process of reasoning or critical thinking. In some items, the speaker's reasoning is flawed. Read each item and select the answer choice that most accurately describes it. Choose **d** if there is no flaw or if the speaker remains neutral.

6. "I can either quit my job or put up with my unpleasant coworker. I have no other choices."
a. The speaker is using circular reasoning.
b. The speaker is committing the slippery slope fallacy.
c. The speaker is committing the no in-between fallacy.
d. There's nothing wrong with the speaker's reasoning.

7. "I'm going to decline her invitation because she might decline mine."
a. The speaker is guilty of making a biased generalization.
b. The speaker is using scare tactics.
c. The speaker is committing the two wrongs make a right fallacy.
d. There's nothing wrong with the speaker's reasoning.

8. "The only time I tried that Indian restaurant I got an upset stomach. That place is awful!"
a. The speaker is using the straw man argument.
b. The speaker is making a hasty generalization.
c. The speaker's evidence is not compatible with existing knowledge.
d. There's nothing wrong with the speaker's reasoning.

9. "I am tired because I didn't get any sleep last night."
a. The speaker is using circular reasoning.
b. The speaker is not providing credible evidence.
c. The speaker's argument is a tentative truth.
d. There's nothing wrong with the speaker's explanation.

10. "He's got almost all of the credentials we are looking for, but I don't think we should hire him—he's a Democrat."
a. The speaker is committing the *ad hominem* fallacy.
b. The speaker is presenting the chicken or egg dilemma.
c. This is a *post hoc* fallacy.
d. There's nothing wrong with the speaker's reasoning.

Read the following passage carefully and then answer the questions that follow.

Anna's apartment has been robbed. Only her valuable jewels, which she kept carefully hidden, have been stolen. Anna claims that the only people who knew where the jewels were hidden were her mother and her fiancée, Louis. Anna recently lost her job. Louis claims he was working at the time of the robbery and that he never told anyone else about the hiding place. Louis's boss and a coworker vouch for Louis, claiming he was indeed at work at the time of the robbery. However, Louis's boss was not with Louis the entire time—he left before Louis's shift was over. Louis's boss was convicted of insurance fraud several years ago. Anna's insurance on the jewelry is worth several hundred thousand dollars. She recently had the jewels reappraised.

11. Which of the following is the most logical conclusion to draw from the above evidence?

   a. Anna fabricated the whole thing for the insurance money.

   b. Louis stole the jewels and is paying his boss to cover for him.

   c. Anna, Louis, and Louis's boss are all in it together for the insurance money.

   d. Anna is an innocent victim of a plot by Louis and his boss to steal her jewelry and sell it while Louis helps her spend her insurance money.

12. Is Louis's boss's testimony credible? Why or why not?

Answers

1. The answer is **c**, slippery slope. Notice how the passage claims that if *X* happens ("if we don't act now"), then *Y* will automatically follow ("there will soon be thousands of companies destroying our world's most bountiful gardens"). But not putting a stop to tropical deforestation now doesn't necessarily mean that, for example, the habitat of indigenous tribes of people will be destroyed.

2. The correct choice is **b**, dysphemism. "Deadly gas" is a much more negative term than the one it replaces, the more neutral term "carbon monoxide."

3. The correct choice is **d**, biased question. The way the question is phrased makes it difficult to answer "yes."

4. The correct choice is **d**, all of the above.

5. Since the statistic cited in the passage can't be accepted as fact, then the passage doesn't contain any credible facts. The statistic can be accepted as a tentative truth until more information is given.

6. The correct choice is **c**, the no in-between fallacy. The speaker is not considering that there are more options. He or she, for example, could talk to the coworker directly or to the department supervisor about the situation.

7. The correct choice is **c**; the speaker is committing the two wrongs make a right fallacy. The speaker is assuming that it is acceptable to do something to someone else because that person might be planning on doing that same thing to you.

8. The correct choice is **b**, the speaker is making a hasty generalization. The speaker is making a conclusion based on too little evidence.

9. The correct choice is **d**, there's nothing wrong with the speaker's reasoning. The speaker is making a conclusion based good evidence and common sense.

10. The correct choice is **a**, the speaker is committing the *ad hominem* fallacy. The speaker is discrediting the potential employee based on his beliefs, not on what he is capable of contributing.

11. The most logical conclusion to draw from this evidence is **c,** that all three of them are in it together. Anna had recently lost her job, so she might be in need of money. The fact that she recently had her jewelry reappraised should add to your suspicions, as should the fact that only the jewelry was taken. Furthermore, Louis's boss committed insurance fraud in the past, so his credibility should be doubted. It might be inferred that Louis's boss committed the robbery, since he was not with Louis the entire time Louis was at work. Even if Louis's boss didn't actually commit the robbery, chances are good that his boss was somehow involved in planning the theft. It's logical to assume that Louis stayed at work so that he wouldn't be a suspect, and therefore, he needed someone else (like his boss) to commit the actual crime.

12. Louis's boss's testimony should be regarded suspiciously. Because this is probably a case of insurance fraud, and because he was guilty of insurance fraud in the past, he's not a trustworthy witness or alibi.

How did you do? If you got all of the answers correct, congratulations! Good work. If you missed a few, you might want to use the following to guide your review.

If you missed:	Then study:
Question 1	Lesson 12
Question 2	Lesson 6
Question 3	Lesson 6
Question 4	Lesson 18
Question 5	Lesson 3
Question 6	Lesson 12
Question 7	Lesson 12
Question 8	Lesson 16
Question 9	Lesson 17
Question 10	Lesson 13
Question 11	Lessons 15 and 19
Question 12	Lessons 5 and 19

▶ Congratulations!

You've completed 20 lessons and have seen your critical thinking and reasoning skills improve. If you're preparing for a standardized test, check Appendix A, which provides tips on how to prepare for and what to do during tests.

Now it's time to reward yourself for a job well done!

Posttest ▶

If you'd like to gauge how much your critical thinking and reasoning skills have improved from working through this book, try this posttest. Though the questions are different from the pretest, they test the same skills, so you will be able to see how much you've learned. The only key difference between the two tests is that the posttest uses the vocabulary words you've learned throughout this book.

After you complete this test, grade it and then compare your score with your score on the pretest. If your score now is much greater than your pretest score, congratulations—you've profited noticeably from your hard work. If your score shows little improvement, perhaps there are certain chapters you need to review. Do you notice a pattern to the types of questions you got wrong? Whatever you score on this posttest, keep this book around for review and to refer to when you need tips on reasoning skills.

On the next page, there's an answer sheet you can use to fill in your answer choices. Or, if you prefer, simply circle the correct answer underneath the item itself. If the book doesn't belong to you, write the numbers 1–35 on a piece of paper and record your answers there. Take as much time as you need to do this short test. When you finish, check your answers against the answer key that follows this test. Each answer tells you which lesson of this book teaches you about the reasoning strategy in that question.

Good luck!

1.	ⓐ	ⓑ	ⓒ	ⓓ		13.	ⓐ	ⓑ	ⓒ	ⓓ		25.	ⓐ	ⓑ	ⓒ	ⓓ
2.	ⓐ	ⓑ	ⓒ	ⓓ		14.	ⓐ	ⓑ	ⓒ	ⓓ		26.	ⓐ	ⓑ	ⓒ	ⓓ
3.	ⓐ	ⓑ	ⓒ	ⓓ		15.	ⓐ	ⓑ	ⓒ	ⓓ		27.	ⓐ	ⓑ	ⓒ	ⓓ
4.	ⓐ	ⓑ	ⓒ	ⓓ		16.	ⓐ	ⓑ	ⓒ	ⓓ		28.	ⓐ	ⓑ	ⓒ	ⓓ
5.	ⓐ	ⓑ	ⓒ	ⓓ		17.	ⓐ	ⓑ	ⓒ	ⓓ		29.	ⓐ	ⓑ	ⓒ	ⓓ
6.	ⓐ	ⓑ	ⓒ	ⓓ		18.	ⓐ	ⓑ	ⓒ	ⓓ		30.	ⓐ	ⓑ	ⓒ	ⓓ
7.	ⓐ	ⓑ	ⓒ	ⓓ		19.	ⓐ	ⓑ	ⓒ	ⓓ		31.	ⓐ	ⓑ	ⓒ	ⓓ
8.	ⓐ	ⓑ	ⓒ	ⓓ		20.	ⓐ	ⓑ	ⓒ	ⓓ		32.	ⓐ	ⓑ	ⓒ	ⓓ
9.	ⓐ	ⓑ	ⓒ	ⓓ		21.	ⓐ	ⓑ	ⓒ	ⓓ		33.	ⓐ	ⓑ	ⓒ	ⓓ
10.	ⓐ	ⓑ	ⓒ	ⓓ		22.	ⓐ	ⓑ	ⓒ	ⓓ		34.	ⓐ	ⓑ	ⓒ	ⓓ
11.	ⓐ	ⓑ	ⓒ	ⓓ		23.	ⓐ	ⓑ	ⓒ	ⓓ		35.	ⓐ	ⓑ	ⓒ	ⓓ
12.	ⓐ	ⓑ	ⓒ	ⓓ		24.	ⓐ	ⓑ	ⓒ	ⓓ						

► Posttest

Read the following passage and then answer the questions that follow.

Joshua's 10-year-old stereo system has just died. He wants to buy a new one, but isn't sure what kind to get. He's on a tight budget but wants good quality—something that will last him for years. He has a large tape collection, but for the last several months, he's bought only CDs because he believes the quality is much better.

1. Which of the following most accurately presents the issues Joshua must consider, in order of priority?
   a. cost, quality, and brand name of system
   b. quality, cost, and components of system
   c. components, quality, and warranty for system
   d. trade-in value of old system and components of new system

2. Which of the following is probably the best choice for Joshua?
   a. a medium-quality stereo with CD player but no tape deck, regular price
   b. a high-quality stereo with a tape deck but no CD, regular price
   c. a high-quality stereo with CD player but no tape deck on sale for half price
   d. a low-quality stereo with CD player and tape deck, sale price

Choose the best answer for each of the following.

3. "These are the most beautiful paintings in the entire museum" is
   a. a fact.
   b. an opinion.
   c. a tentative truth.
   d. none of the above.

4. "The Liberty Bell has three cracks in it" is
   a. a fact.
   b. an opinion.
   c. a tentative truth.
   d. none of the above.

The following items (5–20) present questions, statements, or short passages that illustrate the process of reasoning or critical thinking. In some items, the speaker's reasoning is flawed. Read each item and select the answer choice that most accurately describes it. Choose **d** if there is no flaw or if the speaker remains neutral.

5. "He's been known to embellish the truth on occasion."
   a. "Embellish the truth" is a euphemism.
   b. "Embellish the truth" is a dysphemism.
   c. "On occasion" is vague.
   d. There's nothing wrong with the speaker's reasoning.

6. "Do you support raising the tuition for state schools, making it even harder for the underprivileged to receive an education?"
   a. The question uses circular reasoning.
   b. The question is presenting the *post hoc, ergo propter hoc* fallacy.
   c. The question is biased.
   d. The speaker is remaining neutral.

7. "Give her a chance, Carl. She's a good person, and she's had a really hard time since her mother died. She's never worked in an office before, but you'll be giving her the first break she's had in a long time."
   a. The speaker is using peer pressure.
   b. The speaker is appealing to Carl's sense of pity.
   c. The speaker is using a red herring.
   d. The speaker is remaining neutral.

8. "What does he know? He's a Republican."
   a. The speaker is presenting a straw man.
   b. The speaker is asking a loaded question.
   c. The speaker is presenting an *ad hominem* argument.
   d. There's nothing wrong with the speaker's reasoning.

9. "Tough-Scrub is tougher on dirt!"
   a. The ad is making an incomplete claim.
   b. The ad is appealing to our vanity.
   c. The claim the ad makes is untestable.
   d. There's nothing wrong with this ad.

10. "None of us is going to vote to make the employee lounge a nonsmoking area, so neither are you, right?"
   a. The speaker is presenting a no in-betweens argument.
   b. The speaker is using circular reasoning.
   c. The speaker is using peer pressure.
   d. The speaker is remaining neutral.

11. "I was going so fast, Officer, because I was in a hurry."
   a. The speaker is appealing to vanity.
   b. The speaker is using circular reasoning.
   c. The speaker is reversing cause and effect.
   d. There's nothing wrong with the speaker's explanation.

12. "The average employee works only 45 hours a week and takes home $65,000 a year in salary. Not bad, eh?"
   a. The speaker has made a hasty generalization.
   b. The speaker has committed a *non sequitur*.
   c. The speaker's use of averages could be misleading.
   d. There's nothing wrong with the speaker's reasoning.

13. "If you have sinus trouble, you should try acupuncture. I had sinus troubles for years, and since I've been going to the acupuncturist for the last six months, I can breathe better, sleep better, and I have more energy. And it's painless."
   a. The speaker is using peer pressure.
   b. The speaker is presenting a circular explanation.
   c. The speaker is making a hasty generalization.
   d. There's nothing wrong with the speaker's reasoning.

14. "So the end result is that we either have to cut jobs or go out of business."
   a. The speaker has presented a no in-betweens fallacy.
   b. The speaker has presented a straw man.
   c. The speaker has presented a slippery slope scenario.
   d. There's nothing wrong with the speaker's reasoning.

15. "Music is based on numbers. I'm good with numbers, so I'd be a good musician."
   a. The speaker has committed a *non sequitur*.
   b. The speaker has committed an *ad hominem* fallacy.
   c. The speaker has made a biased generalization.
   d. There's nothing wrong with the speaker's reasoning.

16. "The reason healthcare is in such a problematic state is because the insurance companies are only out to make money."
a. This speaker uses an argument that presents the straw man fallacy.
b. This speaker provides a statistic based on common sense.
c. This speaker presents the slippery slope scenario.
d. There's nothing wrong with the speaker's reasoning.

17. "I have succeeded because I was destined to succeed."
a. The speaker is presenting a circular explanation.
b. The speaker is presenting an untestable explanation.
c. The speaker is reversing cause and effect.
d. There's nothing wrong with the speaker's reasoning.

18. "If you stop going to the gym, the next thing you know, you'll start eating unhealthy food, and before you know it, you'll have heart disease."
a. The speaker is appealing to the listener's sense of pity.
b. The speaker is using flattery.
c. The speaker is presenting a slippery slope argument.
d. There's nothing wrong with the speaker's reasoning.

19. "I know you're concerned about whether or not I inappropriately allocated funds. But what you really should be worrying about is what Senator Hinckley is doing with his illegal campaign contributions!"
a. The speaker is presenting a red herring.
b. The speaker is committing an *ad hominem*.
c. The speaker is using peer pressure.
d. The speaker is remaining neutral.

20. "Hey, Beth, have you tried the new restaurant on our street? I received their flyer in the mail and the place looks amazing!"
a. The speaker's argument is untestable.
b. The speaker is making a hasty generalization.
c. The speaker is using a euphemism.
d. There's nothing wrong with the speaker's reasoning.

In the following situations, which source is most credible?

21. You want to find out about the condition of a used pick-up truck you're thinking of buying.
a. the truck's owner
b. a friend who refurbishes used cars and trucks
c. a used-car salesman
d. an independent garage mechanic

22. You want to find out about the quality of goods in an antique store.
a. a friend who shops there all the time
b. the store's owner
c. an antique specialist
d. a local historian

Read the following argument carefully and answer the questions that follow.

(1) School should be in session year-round rather than just September through June. (2) Having the summer months off means that children spend the first two months at the beginning of the school year reviewing what they learned the year before. (3) This is a waste of precious time. (4) Imagine how much more children would learn if they had an extra four months a year to learn new material. (5) In addition, with so many single-parent households or families where both parents have to work, child care in the long summer months is a serious financial burden on families. (6) Those who can't afford child care have no choice but to leave their children alone.

23. What is the main point (conclusion) of the argument?
a. sentence 1
b. sentence 2
c. sentence 3
d. sentence 4
e. sentence 5

24. This conclusion is
a. a fact.
b. an opinion.
c. a tentative truth.

25. How many major premises support this conclusion?
a. one
b. two
c. three
d. four

26. Which of the following would most strengthen this argument?
a. "Teachers across the country agree."
b. "According to a *New York Times* survey, just one week of summertime child care costs an average of $250."
c. "At least we should make summer camps more affordable and educational."
d. "Studies show that children who read throughout the summer do better in the next school year."

27. Sentence 6 commits which of the following fallacies?
a. red herring
b. straw man
c. no in-betweens
d. *non sequitur*

Read the following passages carefully and answer the questions that follow.

Every day for the last six weeks, LeeAnne has been doing yoga before work in the morning. Since then, she has noticed that she is more relaxed. She has also been given an award for her dedication at work and been asked out on several dates. Furthermore, she has noticed an increase in her appetite.

28. Which of the following is very likely to be the result of her yoga?
   a. She is more relaxed.
   b. She is being asked out on dates.
   c. She has gotten an award at work.
   d. a and c

29. If LeeAnne were to claim that her social life has improved because of her yoga, which of the following would be true?
   a. She'd be making a hasty generalization.
   b. She'd be committing the *post hoc, ergo propter hoc* fallacy.
   c. She'd be reversing cause and effect.
   d. She wouldn't be committing any logical fallacies.

Rhonda wants to plant a flower garden in her yard. She knows she needs to do each of the following:
   1. Decide which flowers she likes best.
   2. Find out which flowers grow best in her climate.
   3. Buy gardening equipment.
   4. Design the flower garden.

30. In which order should Rhonda take the steps listed above?
   a. 1, 2, 3, 4
   b. 4, 3, 2, 1
   c. 2, 1, 3, 4
   d. 2, 1, 4, 3

You would like to know whether the employees in your company have started exercising as a result of the company recently building a new health club on the tenth floor of your building. You get a list of all the employees that received photo identification permitting entrance into the gym. You see that 64 percent of the employees applied for the gym photo ID and therefore conclude that 64 percent of the employees have started to incorporate exercise into their lifestyle as a result of the opening of the new gym.

31. What is wrong with your conclusion?
   a. You haven't found out what kind of exercise the employees are engaging in.
   b. You don't find out whether some, or all, of the employees were exercising elsewhere before the new gym opened.
   c. You don't take into account that just because 64 percent applied for a gym ID, they are not all actually going to the gym.
   d. both **b** and **c**

32. Which of the following could you logically conclude from your before/after comparison?
   a. Sixty-four percent of the employees intended to use the new gym.
   b. Providing a health club for employees improves work performance.
   c. When people have a health club in their place of employment, they are more likely to eat right.
   d. If the gym offered exercise classes, then more people would use it.

33. If you wanted to survey people in your company about the new health club and how it has *changed* or *affected* their lifestyle, which people would provide you with a representative sample?
   a. people who worked for the company before, during, and after the health club was built
   b. people who joined the company after the health club was built
   c. people who never worked for the company
   d. people who belong to a health club

Michelle has a list of chores she needs to get done before 5:00 P.M. She needs to vacuum, but she can't do that between 10–12 or 2–4 because the baby will be sleeping. She needs to do yesterday's dishes, but she can't do that between 9–10 or 12–1 because she and the baby will be eating. She needs to cook dinner, but she can't do that until she does yesterday's dishes, and she wants to do that as close to dinnertime as possible. She also needs to dust, but she wants to do that before she vacuums.

34. Which of the following is the best schedule for Michelle?

	10:00–12:00	1:00–2:00	2:00–4:00	4:00–5:00
a.	vacuum	dust	cook	dishes
b.	dust	vacuum	dishes	cook
c.	dust	dishes	vacuum	cook
d.	dishes	cook	dust	vacuum

Brenda is hosting a dinner party. On one side of the table, Ed *(E)* is sitting next to Mary *(M)*. There are two seats between Annabelle *(A)* and Mary. Annabelle is next to Carl *(C)*. Carl is one seat away from Mary. Roger *(R)* is at one end of the table.

35. In which order are these guests sitting?
  a. *R, A, C, E, M*
  b. *R, C, M, E, A*
  c. *E, M, A, C, R*
  d. *M, C, R, A, E*

▶ Answer Key

You can find relevant instruction and examples for any items you miss in the lesson(s) listed to the right of each correct answer.

1. b. Lesson 2
2. c. Lesson 2
3. b. Lesson 3
4. c. Lesson 3
5. a. Lesson 6
6. c. Lesson 6
7. b. Lesson 11
8. c. Lesson 13
9. a. Lesson 5
10. c. Lesson 11
11. b. Lesson 12
12. c. Lesson 5
13. d. Lessons 7–9
14. a. Lesson 12
15. a. Lessons 15, 16
16. a Lesson 13
17. b. Lesson 14
18. c. Lesson 12

19. a. Lesson 13
20. b. Lessons 15, 16
21. d. Lesson 4
22. c. Lesson 4
23. a. Lesson 7
24. b. Lesson 3
25. b. Lesson 7
26. b. Lessons 7–9
27. c. Lesson 12
28. a. Lessons 15, 17
29. b. Lesson 17
30. d. Lessons 2, 19
31. d. Lessons 15, 18, 19
32. a. Lessons 15, 18, 19
33. a. Lesson 18
34. b. Lessons 15, 19
35. a. Lessons 15, 19

APPENDIX:
How to Prepare for a Test

Most of us get nervous about tests, especially standardized tests, where our scores can have a significant impact on our future. Nervousness is natural—and it can even be an advantage if you know how to channel it into positive energy.

The following pages provide suggestions for overcoming test anxiety both in the days and weeks before the test and during the test itself.

▶ Two to Three Months before the Test

The number one best way to combat test anxiety is to **be prepared.** That means two things: Know what to expect on the test and review the material and skills on which you will be tested.

Know What to Expect

What knowledge or skills will the exam test? What are you expected to know? What skills will you be expected to demonstrate? What is the format of the test? Multiple choice? True or false? Essay? If possible, go to a bookstore or to the library and get a study guide that shows you what a sample test looks like. Or maybe the agency that's testing you for a job gives out a study guide or conducts study sessions. The fewer surprises you have on test day, the better you will perform. The more you know what to expect, the more confident you will be to handle the questions.

Review the Material and Skills You'll Be Tested On

The fact that you are reading this book means that you've already taken this step in regard to logic and reasoning questions. Now, are there other steps you can take? Are there other subject areas that you need to review? Can you make more improvement in this or other areas? If you are really nervous or if it has been a long time since you reviewed these subjects and skills, you may want to buy another study guide, sign up for a class in your neighborhood, or work with a tutor.

The more you know about what to expect on test day and the more comfortable you are with the material and skills to be tested, the less anxious you will be and the better you will do on the test itself.

▶ The Days before the Test

Review, Don't Cram

If you have been preparing and reviewing in the weeks before the exam, there's no need to cram a few days before the exam. Cramming is likely to confuse you and make you nervous. Instead, schedule a relaxed review of all that you have learned.

Physical Activity

Get some exercise in the days preceding the test. You'll send some extra oxygen to your brain and allow your thinking performance to peak on the day you take the test. Moderation is the key here. You don't want to exercise so much that you feel exhausted, but a little physical activity will invigorate your body and brain. Walking is a terrific, low-impact, energy-building form of exercise.

Balanced Diet

Like your body, your brain needs the proper nutrients to function well. Eat plenty of fruits and vegetables in the days before the test. Foods high in lecithin, such as fish and beans, are especially good choices. Lecithin is a protein your brain needs for peak performance. You may even consider a visit to your local pharmacy to buy a bottle of lecithin tablets several weeks before your test.

Rest

Get plenty of sleep the nights before you take the test. Don't overdo it, though, or you'll make yourself as groggy as if you were overtired. Go to bed at a reasonable time, early enough to get the number of hours you need to function **effectively**. You'll feel relaxed and rested if you've gotten plenty of sleep in the days before you take the test.

Trial Run

At some point before you take the test, make a trial run to the testing center to see how long it takes you to get there. Rushing raises your emotional energy and lowers your intellectual capacity, so you want to allow plenty of time on test day to get to the testing center. Arriving ten or fifteen minutes early gives you time to relax and get situated.

Motivation

Plan some sort of celebration—with family or friends, or just by yourself—for after the test. Make sure it's something you'll really look forward to and enjoy. If you have something to look forward to after the test is over, you may find it easier to prepare and keep moving during the test.

▶ Test Day

It's finally here, the day of the big test. Set your alarm early enough to allow plenty of time to get to the testing center. Eat a good breakfast. Avoid anything that's really high in sugar, such as donuts. A sugar high turns into a sugar low after an hour or so. Cereal and toast, or anything with complex carbohydrates is a good choice. Eat only moderate amounts. You don't want to take a test feeling stuffed! Your body will channel its energy to your digestive system instead of your brain.

Pack a high-energy snack to take with you. You may have a break sometime during the test when you can grab a quick snack. Bananas are great. They have a moderate amount of sugar and plenty of brain nutrients, such as potassium. Most proctors won't allow you to eat a snack while you're testing, but a peppermint shouldn't pose a problem. Peppermints are like smelling salts for your brain. If you lose your concentration or suffer from a momentary mental block, a peppermint can get you back on track. Don't forget the earlier advice about relaxing and taking a few deep breaths.

Leave early enough so you have plenty of time to get to the test center. Allow a few minutes for unexpected traffic. When you arrive, locate the restroom and use it. Few things interfere with concentration as much as a full bladder. Then find your seat and make sure it's comfortable. If it isn't, tell the proctor and ask to move to something you find more suitable.

Now relax and think positively! Before you know it, the test will be over, and you'll walk away knowing you've done as well as you can.

▶ Combating Test Anxiety

Okay—you know what the test will be on. You've reviewed the subjects and practiced the skills on which you will be tested. So why do you still have that sinking feeling in your stomach? Why are your palms sweaty and your hands shaking?

Even the brightest, most well-prepared test takers sometimes suffer bouts of test anxiety. But don't worry; you can overcome it. Below are some specific strategies to help you.

Take the Test One Question at a Time

Focus all your attention on the one question you're answering. Block out any thoughts about questions you've already read or concerns about what's coming next. Concentrate your thinking where it will do the most good—on the question you're answering now.

Develop a Positive Attitude

Keep reminding yourself that you're prepared. In fact, if you've read this book or any other in the Learning-Express Skill Builder series, you're probably better prepared than most other test takers. Remember, it's only a test, and you're going to do your **best**. That's all anyone can ask of you. If that nagging drill sergeant voice inside your head starts sending negative messages, combat them with positive ones of your own. Tell yourself:

- "I'm doing just fine."
- "I've prepared for this test."
- "I know exactly what to do."
- "I know I can get the score I'm shooting for."

You get the idea. Remember to drown out negative messages with positive ones of your own.

If You Lose Your Concentration

Don't worry about it! It's normal. During a long test, it happens to everyone. When your mind is stressed or overexerted, it takes a break whether you want it to or not. It's easy to get your concentration back if you simply acknowledge the fact that you've lost it and take a quick break. You brain needs very little time (seconds, really) to rest.

Put your pencil down and close your eyes. Take a deep breath, hold it for a moment, and let it out slowly. Listen to the sound of your breathing and repeat this two more times. The few seconds this takes is really all the time your brain needs to relax and get ready to refocus. This exercise also helps control your heart rate, so that you can keep anxiety at bay.

Try this technique several times in the days before the test when you feel stressed. The more you practice, the better it will work for you on test day.

If You Freeze

Don't worry about a question that stumps you even though you're sure you know the answer. Mark it and go on to the next question. You can come back to the "stumper" later. Try to put it out of your mind completely until you come back to it. Just let your subconscious mind chew on the question while your conscious mind focuses on the other items (one at a time—of course). Chances are, the memory block will be gone by the time you return to the question.

If you freeze before you even begin the test, here's what to do:

1. Do some deep breathing to help yourself relax and focus.
2. Remind yourself that you're prepared.
3. Take a little time to look over the test.
4. Read a few of the questions.
5. Decide which ones are the easiest and start there.

Before long, you'll be "in the groove."

▶ Time Strategies

One of the most important—and nerve-wracking—elements of a standardized test is time. You'll only be allowed a certain number of minutes for each section, so it is very important that you use your time wisely.

Pace Yourself

The most important time strategy is **pacing yourself**. Before you begin, take just a few seconds to survey the test, making note of the number of questions and of the sections that look easier than the rest. Then, make a rough time schedule based on the amount of time available to you. Mark the halfway point on your test and make a note beside that mark of what the time will be when the testing period is half over.

Keep Moving

Once you begin the test, **keep moving**. If you work slowly in an attempt to make fewer mistakes, your mind will become bored and begin to wander. You'll end up making far more mistakes if you're not concentrating. Worse, if you take too long to answer questions that stump you, you may end up running out of time before you finish.

So don't stop for difficult questions. Skip them and move on. You can come back to them later if you have time. A question that takes you five seconds to answer counts as much as one that takes you several minutes, so pick up the easy points first. Besides, answering the easier questions first helps build your confidence and gets you in the testing groove. Who knows? As you go through the test, you may even stumble across some relevant information to help you answer those tough questions.

Don't Rush

Keep moving, but **don't rush.** Think of your mind as a seesaw. On one side is your emotional energy. On the other side is your intellectual energy. When your emotional energy is high, your intellectual capacity is low. Remember how difficult it is to reason with someone when you're angry? On the other hand, when your intellectual energy is high, your emotional energy is low. Rushing raises your emotional energy and reduces your intellectual capacity. Remember the last time you were late for work? All that rushing around probably caused you to forget important things—like your lunch. Move quickly to keep your mind from wandering, but don't rush and get yourself flustered.

Check Yourself

Check yourself at the halfway mark. If you're a little ahead, you know you're on track and may even have a little time left to check your work. If you're a little behind, you have several choices. You can pick up the pace a little, but do this *only* if you can do it comfortably. Remember—**don't rush!** You can also skip around in the remaining portion of the test to pick up as many easy points as possible. This strategy has one drawback, however. If you are marking a bubble-style answer sheet and you put the right answers in the wrong bubbles—they're wrong. So pay close attention to the question numbers if you decide to do this.

▶ Avoiding Errors

When you take the test, you want to make as few errors as possible in the questions you answer. Here are a few tactics to keep in mind.

Control Yourself

Remember that comparison between your mind and a seesaw? Keeping your emotional energy low and your intellectual energy high is the best way to avoid mistakes. If you feel stressed or worried, stop for a few seconds. Acknowledge the feeling (Hmmm! I'm feeling a little pressure here!), take a few deep breaths, and send yourself some positive messages. This relieves your emotional anxiety and boosts your intellectual capacity.

Directions

In many standardized testing situations, a proctor reads the instructions aloud. Make certain you understand what is expected. If you don't, **ask.** Listen carefully for instructions about how to answer the questions and make certain you know how much time you have to complete the task. Write the time on your test if you don't already know how long you have to take the test. If you miss this vital information, **ask for it.** You need it to do well on your test.

Answers

This may seem like a silly warning, but it is important. Place your answers in the right blanks or the corresponding ovals on the answer sheet. Right answers in the wrong place earn no points—they may even lose you points. It's a good idea to check every five to ten questions to make sure you're in the right spot. That way, you won't need much time to correct your answer sheet if you have made an error.

Logic and Judgement Questions

Standardized tests often feature a section designed to test your judgement, common sense, or logic. Often, these questions are based on a hypothetical situation, which may be presented in a separate paragraph or as part of the question. Here are a few tactics for approaching such questions.

This may seem strange, but a few questions can be answered without reading the passage. If the passage is short (four sentences or so), read the questions first. You may be able to answer them by using your common sense. You can check your answers later after you've actually read the passage. If you're unsure, though, *don't guess;* read the passage carefully. If you can't answer any of the questions, you still know what to look for in the passage. This focuses your reading and makes it easier for you to retain important information. If you know what to look for ahead of time, it's easier to find the information.

Questions based on a hypothetical situation actually test your reading ability as much as your logic and common sense. So be sure you read the situation carefully. **Circle** information that tells who, what, when, or where. The circles will be easy to locate later if you come across a question that asks for specific information. Marking up a passage in this way also heightens your concentration and makes it more likely that you'll remember the information when you answer the questions following the passage. Be sure to read the questions and answer choices carefully, too. A simple word like *not* can turn a right answer into a wrong answer.

Choosing the Right Answers by Process of Elimination

Make sure you understand what the question is asking. If you're not sure of what's being asked, you'll never know whether you've chosen the right answer. So figure out what the question is asking. If the answer isn't readily apparent, look for clues in the answer choices. Notice the similarities and differences in the answer choices. Sometimes, this helps put the question in a new perspective and makes it easier to answer. If you're still not sure of the answer, use the process of elimination. First, eliminate any answer choices that are obviously wrong. Then, reason your way through the remaining choices. You may be able to use relevant information from other parts of the test. If you can't eliminate any of the answer choices, you might be better off to skip the question and come back to it later. If you can't eliminate any answer choices to improve your odds when you come back later, then make a guess and move on.

If You're Penalized for Wrong Answers

You **must know** whether there's a penalty for wrong answers before you begin the test. If you don't, ask the proctor before the test begins. Whether you make a guess depends on the penalty. Some standardized tests are scored in such a way that every wrong answer reduces your score by one-fourth or one-half of a point. Whatever the penalty, if you can eliminate enough choices to make the odds of answering the question better than the penalty for getting it wrong, make a guess.

Let's imagine you are taking a test in which each answer has four choices and you are penalized one-fourth of a point for each wrong answer. If you have no clue and cannot eliminate any of the answer choices, you're better off leaving the question blank because the odds of answering correctly are one in four. This makes the penalty and the odds equal. However, if you can eliminate one of the choices, the odds are now in your favor. You have a one in three chance of answering the question correctly. Fortunately, few tests are scored using such elaborate means, but if your test is one of them, know the penalties and calculate your odds before you take a guess on a question.

If You Finish Early

Use any time you have left at the end of the test or test section to check your work. First, make certain you've put the answers in the right places. As you're doing this, make sure you've answered each question only once. Most standardized tests are scored in such a way that questions with more than one answer are marked wrong. If you've erased an answer, make sure you've done a good job. Check for stray marks on your answer sheet that could distort your score.

After you've checked for these obvious errors, take a second look at the more difficult questions. You've probably heard the folk wisdom about never changing an answer. It's not always good advice. If you have a good reason for thinking a response is wrong, change it.

▶ After the Test

Once you've finished, *congratulate yourself.* You've worked hard to prepare; now it's time to enjoy yourself and relax. Remember that celebration you planned before the test? Now it's time to go to it!

NOTES

NOTES

NOTES

Master the Basics... Fast!

If you need to improve your basic skills to move ahead either at work or in the classroom, then our LearningExpress books are designed to help anyone master the skills essential for success. It features 20 easy lessons to help build confidence and skill fast. This series includes real world examples—**WHAT YOU REALLY NEED TO SUCCEED.**

Easy to Use & Understand

All of these books:

- Give quick and easy instruction
- Provides compelling, interactive exercises
- Share practical tips and valuable advise that can be put to use immediately
- Includes extensive lists of resources for continued learning

Achieve Test Success
With LearningExpress

Our acclaimed series of academic and other job related exam guides are the most sought after resources of their kind. Get the edge with the only exam guides to offer the features that test-takers have come to expect from LearningExpress—The Exclusive LearningExpress Advantage:

Easy to Use & Understand

- **THREE** Complete practice tests based on official exams
- Vital review of skills tested and hundreds of sample questions with full answers and explanations
- The exclusive LearningExpress Test Preparation System—must know exam information, test-taking strategies, customized study planners, tips on physical and mental preparation and more.

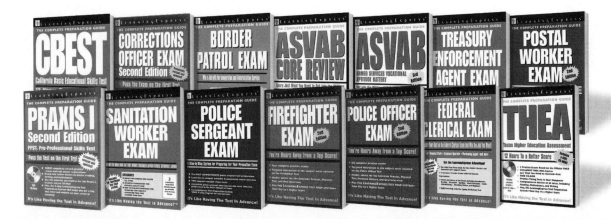